Andrea Queensborough

KU-479-166

The Story
of Britain

Childcraft

The Story of Britain – a **Childcraft** title
Childcraft Reg. US Pat.Off. Marca Registrada

Copyright © 1989 by World Book, Inc.
World Book – Childcraft International Division
World Book House
77 Mount Ephraim
Tunbridge Wells
Kent TN4 8AZ, UK.

This volume may not be reproduced in whole or in part
in any form without written permission from the
publishers.

All rights reserved.

Printed in USA

ISBN 0-7166-6490-9

A/HI

The Story of Britain

World Book, Inc.
a Scott Fetzer company
Chicago London Sydney
Toronto

Managing Editor: Felicia Bailey
Project Editor: Gerry Bailey
Editor: Alice Webb
Author: Tim Wood
Designer: Mike Long
Picture Research: Samantha Bentham

History Consultants: Dr J.S. Morril, MA, D.Phil, FRHS
                      Senior Tutor
                      Selwyn College Cambridge

                      Prof J.R. Vincent, MA, D.Phil, FRHS
                      School of History
                      University of Bristol

Contents

The first Britons

The hunters glided through the forest. Their bare feet hardly made a sound among the dead leaves. The antler head-dresses they wore, cast strange shadows in the pale sunlight. Silently, the group spread out and surrounded the herd of red deer that grazed quietly in the forest clearing.

Suddenly, one of the hunters gave a loud cry. At his signal, the others released their weapons into the herd, bringing three deer to the ground. The rest of the deer fled into the trees. Later, the hunters would skin their prize with sharp stone knives and prepare the meat for cooking.

These hunters were some of the first people to live in Britain. They came from Europe in about 250,000 BC, crossing over a thin strip of marshy land which joined Britain to Europe at that time. The early Britons lived by hunting, and by gathering berries, nuts and roots to eat. They made simple tools and weapons from sharp pieces of flint, a very hard stone which breaks apart easily.

In about 200,000 BC, these hunters were driven out of Britain by the snows and frosts of the Ice Ages. But when the weather became warmer, in about 10,000 BC, people gradually returned to Britain. They brought with them new skills. For example, they made tents out of animal skins and fish traps out of sticks. Most important of all, they knew how to make fire. To do this, they would strike two flints together to make a spark. They used fire to cook their food and to stay warm at night.

Casting in bronze

The smith's face was red and he was sweating. A cool breeze blew, but the heat from the fire was intense. In the fire sat a small pot of liquid bronze, which the smith now lifted carefully with a pair of tongs. Slowly, he poured the metal into a mould, or hollow container, where it would cool. This method of shaping metal was called casting.

The people who lived in Britain in about 2000 BC had learned the art of making tools and weapons out of metal. At first, the smiths used copper metal for this, but even when copper cooled, it wasn't really hard enough. The tools and weapons made from it didn't stay sharp for very long. Then the smiths discovered that, if they added some tin to the copper, they could make a stronger metal. Tools and weapons in this new bronze metal stayed sharper for longer.

We call this period of history the Bronze Age. The Bronze Age people were farmers. They didn't wander about like the very first Britons, but lived in small tribes, or groups, near the fields they farmed.

The Celtic tribes

The first chariots appeared just as the sun was rising. The villagers grabbed their weapons and ran to defend their huts. But the chariots charged down upon them, scattering people in all directions. The warriors in the chariots leaped down, swinging their long iron swords around and stabbing with their sharp spears.

In a few minutes the attack was over. Those villagers who weren't dead had been captured. Huts were blazing all around. The warriors were rounding up the cattle and driving them away to their hill fort.

The warriors were Celts. These fierce tribes had first come to Britain in about 600 BC. They had already conquered much of Europe and were now invading Britain. The Celtic tribes were constantly fighting each other for land and cattle, so each tribe would build itself a huge hill fort for protection. Remains of over three thousand hill forts can be seen in Britain today.

The Celts lived in the period of history known as the Iron Age. They knew how to make fighting weapons of iron, and strong ploughs with iron blades. Most Celts were farmers, not warriors. They lived in small villages and stored their grain in pits. They also kept herds of cattle and sheep.

The Celts were also traders. They made tough wooden boats with leather sails in which they sailed to Europe. Here, they traded hunting dogs, woollen cloaks, corn and slaves, for wine and olive oil.

Boudicca

Boudicca stood proudly in her chariot and gazed around at the huge British army spread before her. As she slowly raised her arms, the soldiers fell silent. Boudicca's speech was full of passion. Hadn't they heard that their enemy was at this moment far away in Wales? Didn't they know they outnumbered the enemy many times over? Didn't they realize there would never be a better time to drive the hated Roman invaders out of Britain?

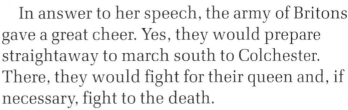

In answer to her speech, the army of Britons gave a great cheer. Yes, they would prepare straightaway to march south to Colchester. There, they would fight for their queen and, if necessary, fight to the death.

The Romans had invaded Britain in AD 43. They had come for two main reasons. They wanted tin, gold, pearls and slaves from Britain. But they also wanted to stop the British Celts, the new generation of Britons, from helping rebellious Celts in other parts of the Roman Empire.

The Romans at first tried to conquer Britain by peaceful means. Some Celtic kings resisted, but they were soon defeated by the well-trained Roman armies, or legions. Soon, much of Britain was under Roman rule.

In AD 61, however, tribes from East Anglia started to fight back. They were led by Boudicca, Queen of the Iceni. She had good reason. Boudicca's father had left his kingdom to the Roman Emperor, Nero, after his death. The Romans had immediately seized the property by force. Boudicca had been whipped and her daughters insulted and badly treated.

Now Boudicca wanted revenge. She gathered together an army and marched south, burning the Roman towns of Colchester, London and St Albans as she went. But then her luck ran out. Her troops were defeated in a battle against the Roman Governor of Britain. And, rather than be captured and made a prisoner, Boudicca took poison and killed herself.

Roman rule

The young Roman officer put down his bottle of oil and picked up a curved bronze scraper. He ran its blunt blade down his arms to remove both the oil and the dirt that he'd gathered on his recent journey. Then he dived into the warm pool for a swim.

The baths were a favourite meeting place for the Romans. Here, they could relax in the steam rooms, the hot baths and in the cold swimming-pool. Here, too, they might exercise at gymnastics or enjoy a wrestling match with each other.

Some time after the Romans invaded Britain, they found hot, natural springs in the south-west of the country. Here they built a number of public baths, which were filled with water from the springs. Later, they built a city on the site. This is known today as Bath. The remains of Roman buildings can still be seen in Bath, as well as in many other cities in Britain.

Roman rule actually brought peace and prosperity to many Britons. They used the Roman market towns as trading centres. The Romans also built powerful forts to defend the new territories they had conquered. And they created hard-wearing roads which ran in straight lines through the British countryside. This meant the Roman soldiers were able to move quickly from one place to another.

In the north, the Romans built Hadrian's Wall to keep out the fierce tribes of Picts. It stretched right across Britain and was defended by many forts.

The Saxon invasion

The sound of axe blows rang through the forest. In the centre of a huge clearing, a group of Saxons were cutting up logs into lengths. They were going to use them to build a settlement, or village, of wooden houses. They would build wooden walls around the settlement, while the ploughmen worked on the land beyond the walls. The largest of the houses would belong to the chief.

The Saxons had come over to Britain when the Romans left the country. Between the years AD 300 and AD 400, the Roman Empire had become steadily weaker. This was caused by plague, civil wars, bad government and attacks from barbarian tribes.

In AD 406, the Romans began to leave Britain in great numbers. And in AD 410, the city of Rome itself was captured by a tribe called the Goths.

Once the last Roman soldiers had left Britain, the people had to fend for themselves. So they hired Saxon soldiers from Germany to help defend them against pirate raids and attacks from the Picts and Scots in the north.

But the Britons soon came to realize that they had made a terrible mistake. The Saxons demanded a lot of money and refused to leave when asked. Instead, they brought over more members of their tribes, who started to build villages and settle down. Before long, other tribes called the Angles, Jutes and Frisians followed them.

Gradually, the last traces of the old Roman way of life vanished. The Britons either joined the Saxons, or fled for safety to the remotest parts of the country, into the lands we now call Wales, Scotland and Cornwall.

The invaders spoke a language which we call 'English'. They settled in Angle-land or 'England'.

The Building of Offa's Dyke

King Offa stood watching the men who were working in the ditch. Thousands of workers cleared away the trees in the area. Some were cutting away the soft, chalky rock, while others filled wicker baskets with rubble. The king nodded with satisfaction. The ditch would mark the boundary of his kingdom.

By AD 600, England was divided into seven kingdoms. Some of the more powerful Saxon chiefs had become kings, and they were often at war with one another.

Map showing the Anglo-Saxon kingdoms

However, no one king was strong enough to overcome all the rest. At first, Northumbria was the most powerful Saxon kingdom. Then, around AD 700, Mercia grew stronger. By AD 900, the kingdom of Wessex led the rest.

King Offa ruled Mercia, which, during his reign, was the most powerful kingdom in Britain. But Offa was troubled by the Britons who kept attacking his kingdom on its border with Wales. He decided to build a deep ditch to mark the western boundary of his lands. This ditch was known as 'Offa's Dyke'. It was an impressive sight. The earth was piled into a wall eight metres high, and any Briton caught crossing it was lucky to escape with his life.

We can still see the names of Saxon kingdoms on maps of England today. Kent, Essex and Sussex are all names of counties. Other Saxon words are also used in British place-names. 'Den' means hill, 'ford' means river-crossing and 'mere' means pool. The word 'dyke' comes from the word 'dik', which means ditch. 'Ton' means a farmstead or village, 'ham' means a homestead, and 'ing' means the place of a family or tribe.

The Christian word

Aidan felt uncomfortable on the horse. He wasn't used to riding and he felt stiff and sore. As he slowed down, looking for somewhere to rest, he noticed a heap of rags lying beside the track. Drawing nearer, he saw that the rags were moving! To his surprise, they were covering a beggar, who was holding out his hand for money!

Aidan slid off his horse and held out the reigns to the beggar, who looked at him in astonishment. The horse must be worth a fortune! Aidan left the animal and strode away, feeling the dust coming through his sandals. He felt better already.

Aidan was the Christian bishop of Northumbria. Everywhere he went, people were amazed by his gentle goodness.

Christianity had almost died out by the time the Saxons invaded Britain. The Saxons were pagans and believed in many gods. One of the few Christians left, a man whom we now call St Patrick, had travelled to Ireland to set up a Christian monastery there. Later, an Irish priest, called Columba, had sailed from Ireland to the west coast of Scotland where he had built another monastery.

Aidan was also spreading the Christian word. He had gone to Northumbria to start a new monastery at Lindisfarne. In AD 595, the Pope sent over missionaries from Rome, led by Augustine. Over the next hundred years, Christianity spread to the whole of the land.

The fury of the Northmen

The Reeve of Dorchester felt nervous. King Brihtric had told him, "Bring the strangers to me". It was a simple enough request. But when the Reeve saw the strangers for himself, he wasn't at all sure his task would be easy.

The strangers leaned on their axes and watched him, scornfully. The Reeve nervously licked his dry lips, then stepped forward to speak. Out of the corner of his eye he caught a flash of sunlight on a sword-blade. His last thought was that these warriors would bring trouble to the land.

These strangers were Vikings from the north. In AD 789, they had sailed southwards to the British Isles in their stout longships from the cold lands of Scandinavia, then returned home again. Four years later, they came back in greater numbers, raiding the monasteries at Lindisfarne and Jarrow on the north-east coast of England.

The Vikings were pagans, so they didn't hesitate to kill any monk who tried to protect his church's treasures. They tore up altars in their search for gold, and left a trail of blazing buildings behind them.

These raids became regular events, and each Viking army seemed to be larger than the one before. Historians at that time wrote of "immense whirlwinds and flashes of lightning and fiery dragons" which seemed to appear before each raid. The Saxons were so terrified of the raiders that they had a special prayer, "God save us from the fury of the Northmen".

A Viking settlement

The town of Jorvik was bustling and noisy as shoppers hurried through the crowded streets. The town craftsmen occupied every spare bit of space. Seated in the open, they carved combs from antlers and bowls from soapstone. They stitched leather shoes and made fine jewellery.

The year was AD 880, and Jorvik, the town now known as York, had become the most important Viking trading centre in Britain. It was nearly a hundred years since the Vikings had first landed, their raids continuing for about seventy years. Then, in AD 851, a huge fleet of over three hundred and fifty ships attacked London. Instead of returning home as usual, the Vikings stayed on for the winter.

Fifteen years later, an even more powerful army landed. This time, the Vikings didn't come to steal, they came to conquer. One by one, the Saxon kingdoms were defeated, until only Wessex remained free.

Many of the Vikings settled in small villages where they began to farm. But the Vikings weren't just fighters and farmers, they were also great traders. Viking ships sailed far and wide. They brought back wine from France, silk from Turkey and Persia, furs from Russia and walrus ivory from Greenland.

Then the Vikings came to Jorvik to trade for the local goods on sale.

King of Wessex

The little Somerset church was chilly. As King
Alfred watched the priest make the sign of the
cross on the Viking's forehead, and bind a
white cloth round his head, he shivered. He
wondered if this simple ceremony would bring
peace to the land we now call England.

Alfred had just defeated the Vikings at the
Battle of Edington. The Vikings had been
forced to make peace and sign a treaty called
the Treaty of Wedmore. And now Guthrum,
their king, was being baptized as a Christian.

Alfred had become King of Wessex in
AD 871, after his brother died. It was a difficult
time to be king. Many Vikings had already
invaded Britain and were settling in the
conquered lands. The Saxons fought them
bravely in many battles but, time after time,
the Vikings won.

Then, in AD 878, the Vikings had attacked
Alfred's palace in the Wessex town of
Chippenham. Alfred had escaped to the island
of Athelney, in the nearby county of Somerset.
Here, surrounded and protected by the
marshes, he had begun to build and train an
army. Soon, it was strong enough to challenge
the Vikings at Edington.

After the battle, the Treaty of Wedmore
divided England between the English and the
Vikings. The English kingdom of Wessex
covered the south and west. The Viking part
of the country was called the Danelaw. It
included what is now Yorkshire, Lincolnshire,
Leicestershire and much of East Anglia.

Alfred was still anxious about the Vikings'
power. He formed a large navy and built many
strong forts along his coastline. Under Alfred's
rule, England became a peaceful and strong
country again.

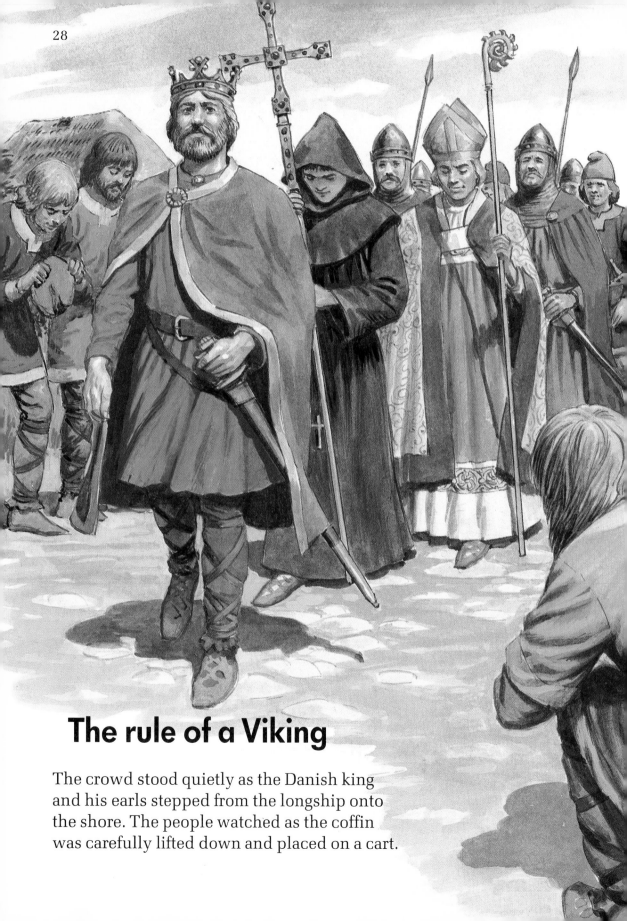

The rule of a Viking

The crowd stood quietly as the Danish king and his earls stepped from the longship onto the shore. The people watched as the coffin was carefully lifted down and placed on a cart.

Then King Cnut and his men formed a procession with the king at the front, and a line of bishops, priests and earls behind. Once the cart had been wheeled into place, the whole procession set off towards Canterbury Cathedral. Here, the body of Archbishop Alfheah was to be buried.

Alfheah had been murdered by Danish Vikings. These were Scandinavian raiders who had terrorized the shores of Britain when Ethelred was king. Ethelred was such a weak king that the Vikings had been able to do almost anything they wanted!

Ethelred was also a poor general. He had tried to persuade the Vikings to leave England by giving them money taken from his subjects in tax. This tax was called the 'Danegeld'. But the Vikings soon realized that if they kept coming back, Ethelred would have to keep paying them to go away again!

At last, in 1016, Ethelred died. The Witan, or Great Council of Earls, elected Cnut of Denmark to be their new king.

Cnut was a Viking, but he was also a Christian. He built many churches in England. And he rebuilt others, such as Canterbury Cathedral, which had previously been destroyed by Viking raiders.

King Cnut was also a fine soldier. He managed to unite the whole of England to fight off any further invasion. And he ruled England wisely, following the laws that had already been laid down.

The Battle of Hastings

It was 1066 and Harold Godwinson, Earl of Wessex, had become King of England. Gaining the throne had not been easy, for Harold had many enemies. He had already fought a great battle against his brother and the Vikings.

Now another strong enemy, William, Duke of Normandy, was threatening him. News had come that William had crossed over from France and was landing on the south coast of England, at Hastings. Harold thought that to stop the French advance, he must march south at once. But here he made a big mistake.

In fact, William had landed with only a small
force of men. If Harold had waited and
strengthened his army first, he might easily
have driven William back. As it was, he had
few archers and no knights on horseback.

The two armies met at Hastings and took up
battle positions. Harold and his Saxon army
were tired, but they took up a strong position
on a hill outside the town and formed a wall
with their shields. They fought well. Then
suddenly, the Norman knights started to run
away. The Saxons chased after them, but the
Norman knights turned and fell on the Saxons
like wolves, cutting them to pieces.

When William saw how successful this trick
had been, he ordered his Norman knights to
repeat it twice more. Then, finally, as evening
drew on, the Norman archers fired a cloud of
arrows into the air and charged again. The wall
of Saxon shields broke apart and Harold, the
last Saxon king of England, was killed.

The Domesday Book

William, Duke of Normandy, was crowned
King of England on Christmas Day, 1066. His
first task as king was to take control of the
country. So he sent his soldiers north to put
down every rebellion they could find there.

← William sent
Commissioners to ask
questions in every village
in England.

Then William gave large amounts of the land
he had conquered from the Saxons to his
Norman barons. In return, each baron had to
rule the land and keep the peace. He also had
to supply soldiers to the king. Many barons
built castles to protect themselves from the
rebellious Saxons.

Then William thought out a plan. In order to
work out what taxes he could raise, he had to
find out how much his land was worth. So he
decided to have a detailed record, or survey,
made of everything he owned.

This survey gave William information about who lived on the land and what the land was used for throughout the whole of England. The results of the survey were written down in a book called the 'Domesday Book'. 'Domesday' means 'Day of Judgement'.

The Domesday Book, which we can still read today, gives us a fascinating picture of what Saxon villages must have looked like in the 11th century. It was even being used at the beginning of the 20th century!

In each village, six people, often the oldest or those with the best memories, formed a jury.

The jury answered questions about their village and the land. ⇗

The Commissioners recorded the answers in the Domesday Book. ⇙

The Commissioners asked the jury of six men questions like these:
How much land is there around the village?
Is the land any good for growing wheat?
How much land cannot be used for farming?
How many ploughs are there in the village?
Is there a mill?
How many pigs, sheep and cows are there?

Cathedrals

The boy stepped nervously off the ladder onto the wooden platform and looked down at the half-finished cathedral below him. He watched, fascinated, as the workmen mixed mortar, lifted blocks of stone and sawed huge timber beams. He thought they looked like tiny ants. The boy's father laughed. "Come on," he said, and held out a mallet and chisel.

The boy was learning to be a stonemason. During the Middle Ages, nineteen grand and majestic cathedrals were built to glorify God. The cathedral at Wells was one of them. The stone for the cathedral was cut from the nearby quarry of Doulting. Great blocks of it were carved into the right shapes to form the arches. As each stone was completed, it was carefully marked to show where it would fit in the building. Coloured glass was put in the windows to form pictures and to tell stories.

Wells Cathedral took over a hundred years to build. Dozens of skilled craftsmen worked on the stone. Some even spent a whole lifetime on the project! A master mason was in charge of the stonemasons. His ability probably meant he was rich and famous.

Hundreds of years later, these magnificent cathedrals still tower over the modern towns which now surround them. When you next visit a cathedral, look carefully at the delicate carving, the soaring arches and the beautiful stained-glass windows inside.

Life in a monastery

It was the young man's seventeenth birthday and he had just finished training to be a Cistercian monk. It was possibly the happiest day of his life. As he knelt in the chapel of Tintern Abbey, on the border of England and Wales, he could hear the River Wye flowing slowly past the monastery. He had never felt so calm and peaceful before.

In the years after the Norman Conquest, many young men chose to join a monastery, while the young women would enter a nunnery. Usually, the monks were almost completely cut off from the outside world. The Cistercians, or White Monks as they were called, deliberately built their monasteries in lonely spots where they would be well away from the temptations of the busier towns.

Rules in the monasteries were strict. Monks were not allowed to possess money, and they couldn't marry. They had to pray seven times a day in the chapel, and the rest of the time they worked in the monastery workshops or fields. Their lives were very simple. They slept on straw mattresses and wore simple, rough woollen clothes called habits.

The monks looked after the poor and helped the sick, and travellers could ask for food and shelter in a monastery overnight. Many monks were scholars, writing books in Latin by hand. Every monastery had its own large library full of books.

King Stephen's reign

A great rock curled through the air and smashed against the castle wall. Almost at once, the archers of King Stephen's army let fly their arrows. The arrows fell like deadly rain onto the high walls and parapets of the castle. The siege had begun.

In the distance, the king's soldiers were setting fire to the villages and fields round about. Smoke from the blazing crops rolled slowly over the terrible scene.

This was civil war. In 1135, King Henry I had died, leaving the throne to his daughter, Matilda. But she had been away in Normandy, France, at the time. Henry's nephew, Stephen, felt he should be king, so he seized the throne while Matilda was away. Civil war broke out between the supporters of the two sides.

Barons from both sides became very powerful during this war. They built strong castles and raised large armies. When they weren't fighting, they were using their soldiers to terrorize the people who lived on the surrounding land.

The barons either raided villages, or demanded money from the villagers in return for not raiding them. They captured prisoners and asked for money for their release.

Stephen tried to shatter the power of
Matilda's barons by attacking their castles and
burning their crops. During the nineteen years
of his troubled reign, the people of England
suffered great misery and hardship.

The young Henry II

"Halt!" King Henry II held up his hand and the long column of wagons and knights came to a standstill. Archers raised their bows and looked nervously at the trees lining the road. Was this an ambush?

Then Henry raised his hunting-horn to his lips and blew a great blast. He spurred his horse into the forest at a gallop, signalling to his barons to follow him. Soon, the most important noblemen in England were racing after their king in hot pursuit of a stag.

Henry II was born in 1133 and became king when he was only twenty-one. He had married Eleanor of Aquitaine, who was a great heiress.

Eleanor had already been married once, to the King of France. By marrying Eleanor, Henry doubled the amount of land in his empire. In fact, he came to rule more lands in France than he did in England.

Henry was an energetic and restless young man. He was also a clever and firm ruler and chose his advisers well. On gaining the throne, his first job was to reduce the power of the barons. To do this, he destroyed hundreds of castles, and peace descended upon the kingdom at last.

Now Henry could turn his attention to governing his people in a good and fair way. He laid down rules about owning property that were to last for hundreds of years.

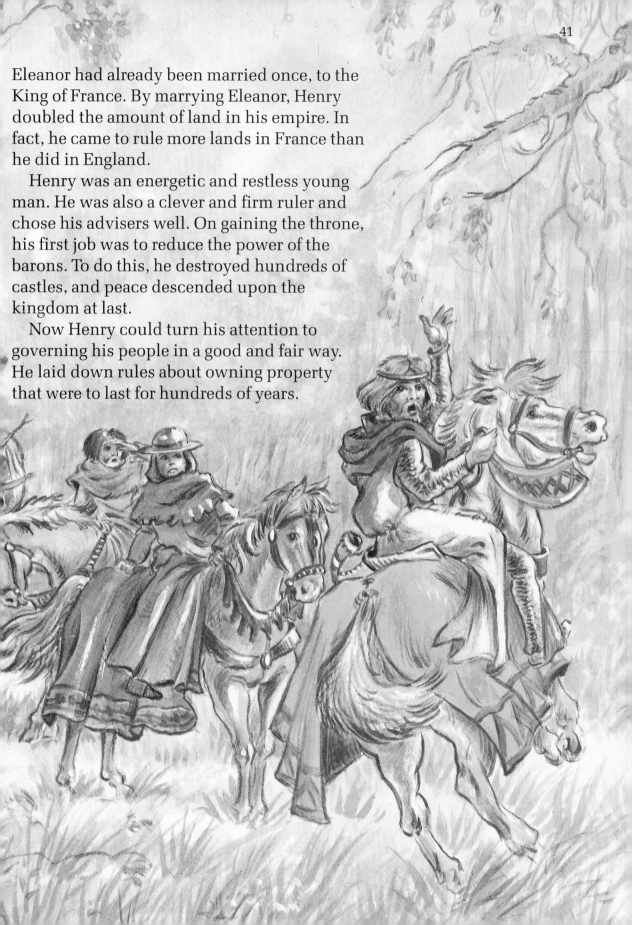

Trial by ordeal

The man staggered and took three more steps before dropping the red-hot iron bar. The pain was terrible! He stared at the burns on the palms of his hands and tried not to cry out. Then a priest hurried forward and wrapped a cloth gently round the man's hands. "God will judge you innocent," he said. And he led him away.

This man had been tried for a crime by a system of judgement called 'trial by ordeal'. This was a harsh system, first used over two hundred years before in the days of King Alfred. If a man was accused of a crime, he had to produce enough witnesses to say he was innocent to be set free. If he couldn't do this, he was tried by ordeal.

In trial by ordeal, the accused person might have to carry a red-hot iron bar for a few paces, or pick a stone out of a cauldron of boiling water with his bare hand. Once the trial was over, the wounds were bandaged up and God was supposed to judge the accused person. If his wounds began to heal in three days, he was innocent. If not, he was guilty.

King Henry II realized how unfair these old methods of judgement were. So he introduced a new system. Travelling judges went round the country, listening to the evidence of the accused person and the witnesses in each case. Trials were also heard by a jury.

In time, Henry built up a whole system of laws, which replaced the local superstitions and customs. At last, ordinary people could get a fair trial in Britain.

Thomas Becket

Thomas Becket clung desperately to a pillar in the cathedral. Then he knelt down on the cathedral floor and tried to pray. As he bowed his head over his hands, the four knights acted swiftly. They drew their swords, which sliced down through the air, and within a few minutes it was all over. Thomas Becket's body lay on the floor in a pool of blood.

Becket had been murdered by Henry II's knights. He had been a friend of Henry's since childhood and, as Chancellor of England, had served him faithfully. But when he was made Archbishop of Canterbury, Becket had quarrelled with the king about a possible new system of law.

Up to 1164, members of the clergy, such as priests and bishops, had been tried in their own religious courts. Because of this, the punishments they were given were not very severe. This meant that any scoundrel who became a clergyman could get away with almost anything. Henry wanted to move cases of serious crimes among the clergy out of the church courts and into the king's courts. But Becket had disagreed.

After much argument, the king's patience had run out and he had shouted furiously, "Will no one rid me of this turbulent priest?" Four of Henry's knights, overhearing the king's words, decided to act upon them. They marched into Becket's room and threatened him. Becket had fled to the cathedral where he thought he would be safe. But the knights had followed him there and killed him.

Henry was so ashamed of the part he had played in Thomas Becket's murder, that he walked barefoot through the snow-covered streets of Canterbury.

An oath of loyalty

The baron knelt in front of the king and raised his sword. "I become your man from this day forward, for life and limb and loyalty," he said. "I shall be true and faithful to you for the lands I hold from you." When he had finished this oath, the baron stood up and bowed. This was how barons gained their power from kings in England during the Middle Ages.

When William the Conqueror became king, he had claimed the whole of England for himself. But he knew that he would find it hard to control the two million Saxons and Vikings who lived there. After all, he only had five thousand knights in his army. So he bought the loyalty of the noblemen who followed him. He gave these barons huge areas of land in return for an oath of loyalty.

In turn, the barons gave some of their land to the knights who had supported them. The knights had to swear to the barons that they would supply them with soldiers if there was ever any need.

The knights divided their lands into estates called 'manors'. They protected the peasants, or 'villeins', who lived there, and allowed them to work on the land. The peasants kept most of what they grew, but in return they had to work for the knight, or 'lord of the manor'. They gave him gifts of produce and paid him taxes.

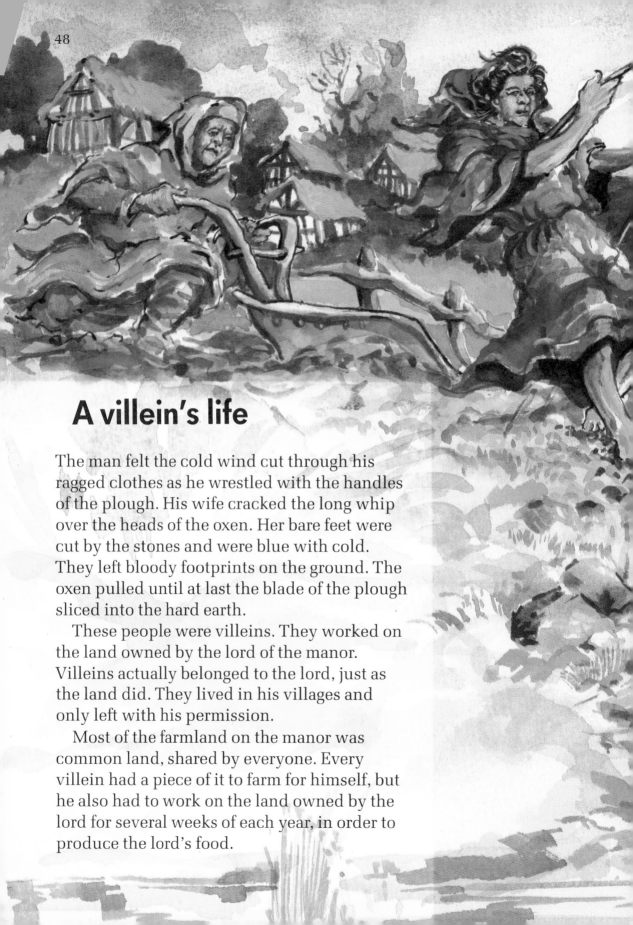

A villein's life

The man felt the cold wind cut through his ragged clothes as he wrestled with the handles of the plough. His wife cracked the long whip over the heads of the oxen. Her bare feet were cut by the stones and were blue with cold. They left bloody footprints on the ground. The oxen pulled until at last the blade of the plough sliced into the hard earth.

These people were villeins. They worked on the land owned by the lord of the manor. Villeins actually belonged to the lord, just as the land did. They lived in his villages and only left with his permission.

Most of the farmland on the manor was common land, shared by everyone. Every villein had a piece of it to farm for himself, but he also had to work on the land owned by the lord for several weeks of each year, in order to produce the lord's food.

The villeins had to perform many other duties and services for the lord. They had to help gather the harvest for him each year, and produce a basket of fresh eggs for him every Easter. If a villein built a hut, or if his daughter got married, he had to pay taxes.

The villeins bought iron and salt from the nearest town, but otherwise they were able to support themselves. They grew all their own food, wore their own cloth and chopped down trees in the forest to provide wood for fuel and for building.

They got up at dawn and worked all day. They ate bread with a thick vegetable soup called pottage, washed down with watery beer. It was a difficult life. There was a lot of disease and many children died at birth. Few villeins, male or female, lived beyond the age of fifty.

Feasts and festivals

The lady of the manor cut the first ears of grain from the stalks of wheat. She was whispering a prayer for her husband who was far away, fighting a war in the Holy Land. She prayed for him to return home safely. All around her, happy children gathered excitedly. "Not long now till the Loaf Mass and the feast!" they cried.

Life for the peasants was hard, but every now and then they would celebrate festivals, and these were happy occasions. One of the most exciting was Lammas, which was held on August 1st after the first harvest had been gathered in. The lord of the manor would invite all the men and their families to take part in a great feast, which he would pay for.

cutting wheat

a Lammas feast

a nativity play

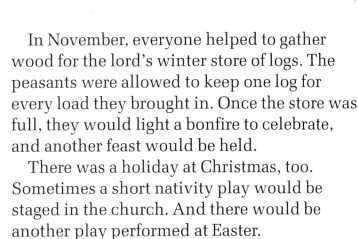

In November, everyone helped to gather wood for the lord's winter store of logs. The peasants were allowed to keep one log for every load they brought in. Once the store was full, they would light a bonfire to celebrate, and another feast would be held.

There was a holiday at Christmas, too. Sometimes a short nativity play would be staged in the church. And there would be another play performed at Easter.

Wandering entertainers sometimes visited the villages, or gathered at one of the great fairs held in the country every year. The entertainers included musicians, jugglers, acrobats and performing animals. The travellers would bring news of the outside world, often causing great excitement among the people of the village.

a fair

Knights of the Cross

It was pouring with rain as the Knights of the
Cross huddled together in a group beside King
Richard. They spoke in anxious voices,
warning the king that the siege of Jerusalem
might take them many months to win. Besides,
another enemy force was already marching
north towards them.

King Richard listened carefully. Then, with
great reluctance, he gave them the order to
retreat. They would have to give up the siege.

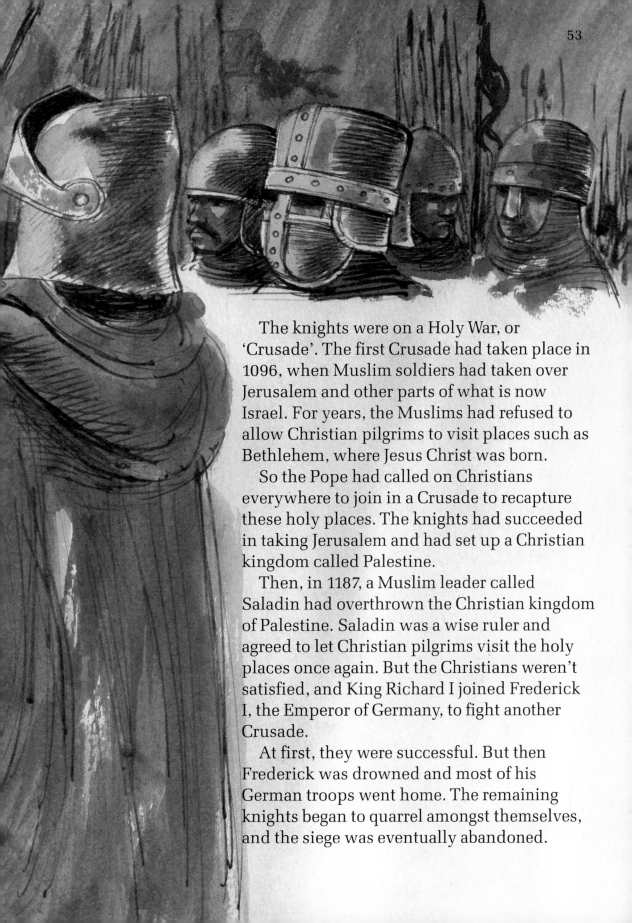

The knights were on a Holy War, or 'Crusade'. The first Crusade had taken place in 1096, when Muslim soldiers had taken over Jerusalem and other parts of what is now Israel. For years, the Muslims had refused to allow Christian pilgrims to visit places such as Bethlehem, where Jesus Christ was born.

So the Pope had called on Christians everywhere to join in a Crusade to recapture these holy places. The knights had succeeded in taking Jerusalem and had set up a Christian kingdom called Palestine.

Then, in 1187, a Muslim leader called Saladin had overthrown the Christian kingdom of Palestine. Saladin was a wise ruler and agreed to let Christian pilgrims visit the holy places once again. But the Christians weren't satisfied, and King Richard I joined Frederick I, the Emperor of Germany, to fight another Crusade.

At first, they were successful. But then Frederick was drowned and most of his German troops went home. The remaining knights began to quarrel amongst themselves, and the siege was eventually abandoned.

The Magna Carta

King John got down from his horse and slowly approached the throne. A table had been set before it, near which stood a crowd of barons and church leaders.

The king sat down and looked at the Great Charter laid out before him. Slowly and reluctantly, he took up the Great Seal of England. Then he pressed it into the hot wax. The Magna Carta had been signed!

King John was not a popular or a successful king. He had quarrelled with the barons, who hated the heavy taxes and fines he made them pay. In the spring of 1215, the barons had captured London and, at Runnymede, on the banks of the River Thames, they forced King John to sign the Magna Carta.

Many of the barons had fought with the King of France against John. During this long war, John had lost Normandy and many other English lands. In fact, he was defeated so many times he was nicknamed 'Softsword'.

John had also caused religious problems in England. He had quarrelled with the Pope, who was Head of the Church, over who should be Archbishop of Canterbury. The Pope was so angry that he had closed all the English churches. For seven years, no one could hold a wedding or a proper funeral in church.

The Magna Carta was a long document. It listed all the things that the barons wanted. Although it really only applied to the barons, it laid down the idea that England should be ruled by proper laws, not just by the whim of the king. The Magna Carta ended unfair taxation and imprisonment without trial.

The Great Parliament

Simon de Montford, the most powerful baron in England, rose proudly to his feet. The crowd of barons, bishops and knights who had been talking among themselves, suddenly fell silent. The Great Parliament had begun.

In 1265, Simon de Montford, Earl of Leicester, had led many of the barons in a revolt against the king, Henry III. He had taken Henry's son, Prince Edward, prisoner. Simon accused the king of bad government and of overtaxing the people, and he forced him to call a 'Parliament' at Westminster.

Simon wanted this Parliament to consist of the king and a group, or council, of advisers. The council would talk freely with the king about laws and taxes, and help him to rule England. Simon believed that having a council would reduce the king's power and force him to rule according to the Magna Carta.

Kings often had advisers to help them rule, but Simon's Parliament was unusual. It contained knights and citizens from the larger towns, as well as rich and powerful lords. This was the first time that some of the ordinary people had been given a chance to offer advice to a king.

But a few months after the Great Parliament met, Prince Edward escaped. He gathered together an army and marched against Simon de Montford, defeating him at the Battle of Evesham. Simon was killed.

The rebellion was over but the ideas behind Simon de Montford's Parliament remained. England had taken the first steps towards government by Parliament.

Craftsmen's guilds

The guild officials picked up the young man's silver cup. This moment would decide his whole future. Would the standard of workmanship be good enough? The young man's heart was pounding with excitement as the officials examined the cup. Then at last they looked at him and smiled. The young man was to be accepted as a member of the silversmiths' guild, after all!

Parents paid a craftsman to take on their son as an apprentice.

The boy learned the skills of the job from the craftsman, and lived in the shop.

As towns developed in the Middle Ages, the craftsmen formed themselves into groups called guilds. Each craft had its own guild, which drew up rules to make sure that its goods were well made, and that the prices charged were neither too high nor too low.

Guild members were forbidden to work in public, in case they gave away the secrets of their trade. They were not allowed to work after dark, which ensured that everyone worked the same number of hours and kept up the same standard of work. People who broke the rules were punished by the guild courts.

No one could practise a craft unless he or she belonged to a guild. Members had to pay to belong and, in return, the guild helped them if they were sick.

The guilds also organized plays, which were performed at festivals. These were usually based on stories from the Bible and were often related to the particular craft of the guild. For example, the Fishmongers' Guild might put on a play about Jonah and the Whale.

After seven years, the apprentice became a journeyman and received his first pay.

To become a master craftsman, the journeyman had to produce a 'masterpiece'.

If his masterpiece was accepted, he was allowed to start work in his own shop.

Learning in Latin

"Hold out your hand!" roared the friar, his face red with anger. "If you don't learn your Latin verbs, I will have to beat them into you!" As the friar scolded the lazy pupil, the other children in the class bent their heads over their wax tablets and scribbled furiously.

During the Middle Ages, children used to go to the monasteries or to the cathedral schools to learn, although some pupils were taught at home. Most of the pupils came from wealthy families, but children who were poor might receive special attention if they were talented, especially if they were going to become monks. The main subject taught in the schools was the classical language of Latin.

The University of Oxford was founded during the 12th century. Students began their university studies at the age of fourteen. Often, they could hardly read at this age. They studied for up to six years to gain a degree, usually in philosophy, or possibly in law or religion. There were no official holidays and students came and went as they pleased. Rich priests were required to pay for the poorest scholars to attend the university.

In 1209, an Oxford student murdered a woman and escaped. Because he was never caught, the Mayor of Oxford ordered that three of the murderer's friends should be hanged in his place! Many protests followed, and a lot of students and teachers left Oxford to set up a new university at Cambridge. Today, almost every important city and town in Britain has its own university.

Mining the walls

At last the branches were stacked in place. "Everybody out!" ordered the sergeant. The soldiers moved as quickly as they could along the chalk tunnel and emerged, blinking, into the sunlight. The sergeant stayed behind to light a bundle of hay, then, as the flames crackled in the branches, he too made his way back to the tunnel entrance.

These men were trying to capture a castle by 'mining the walls'. During the Middle Ages, castles were built with such sturdy walls and stong defences that it became very difficult to capture them by force. An attacking army might try to capture a castle in one of several ways. They might use trickery, they might bribe the defenders to give up, or they might starve them out. But if none of these ways worked, the castle had to be stormed.

Huge catapults were used to hurl rocks at the walls in an attempt to smash large holes in them. Iron-tipped battering rams were swung at the gates. Soldiers swarmed up siege-ladders to attack the defenders on top of the walls. But these methods were slow, and many might be killed.

Another way was to 'mine' the walls. A tunnel would be dug under one section of the wall and the roof of the tunnel propped up with timber. Then a fire was lit inside. The tunnel would collapse, and the section of wall above it would fall in. The only way to prevent 'mining', was to surround the castle with a deep moat filled with water.

Catapults, or stone-throwing machines, were used to batter down castle walls during a siege.

Jousting

The two armoured horsemen galloped at full charge towards one another. Each held out a long weapon, called a lance, in front of him. A long scarf fluttered on the arm of one of the horsemen. The lady who had given him the scarf leaned forward with excitement. She watched as her champion lunged forward with his lance and knocked his opponent out of the saddle.

These horsemen lived in the Middle Ages and were known as knights. They spent many years training to fight. They would enter battle wearing strong armour, called chain mail, made from pieces of metal linked together to form a protective vest.

Even in times of peace, the knights still enjoyed fighting. They would take part in practice fights called tournaments. Tournaments were exciting events. People travelled a long way to watch. Even though the knights had to follow strict rules, many were often killed by accident.

Ladies from the royal court would present their favourite knight with a glove or scarf to wear on his lance or arm. These 'favours' were supposed to bring the knight honour.

Any knight who won his fight, or 'joust', was allowed to keep the losing knight's horse and armour. Sometimes, many knights fought at the same time in a 'melée'. The winner was the last knight to remain seated on his horse.

Prince of Wales

King Edward I stood on the battlements of Carnarvon Castle, holding his baby son in his arms. Then he lifted up the child for all to see. "Here is your new Prince of Wales," he cried, "just as I promised you! He was born in Wales, and does not speak a word of English!"

Edward had wanted to give the Welsh a prince, but they wouldn't accept an Englishman who didn't speak Welsh. So Edward solved the problem by offering his son. The young prince had been born in Wales and was too young to speak at all!

England's troubles with the Welsh had started more than two hundred years before. The Normans had built castles along the Welsh borders, or 'marches', to keep the Welsh tribes in check. They had then made daring raids into Wales to steal cattle. The Welsh had never forgotten this.

During the late 13th century, the brave Welsh leader called Llewellyn ap Gryffydd, also known as 'Llewellyn the Last', united the Welsh people in a rebellion against England. He won many victories, earning the right to call himself 'Prince of Wales'.

Llewellyn ap Gryffydd led a Welsh rebellion against the English.

But when Edward I came to the English throne in 1272, Llewellyn knew that he had met a clever opponent. Edward invaded Wales, and Llewellyn was defeated and killed.

This was the end of Llewellyn's rebellion. Wales came under English rule and Edward I built some immense castles. Edward's son became Prince of Wales. And ever since then, the title 'Prince of Wales' has passed to the eldest son of the English monarch.

Owen Glendower

The Welsh nobleman sprang to his feet.
"We must fight the English!" he cried. The
Welshmen who sat around the huge table
raised their flagons and cheered. Owen
Glendower would be their leader!

Owen had once fought in the English army
against the Scots. But a quarrel with an
Englishman over a piece of land had made him
so angry that he had decided to fight for
Wales's independence instead.

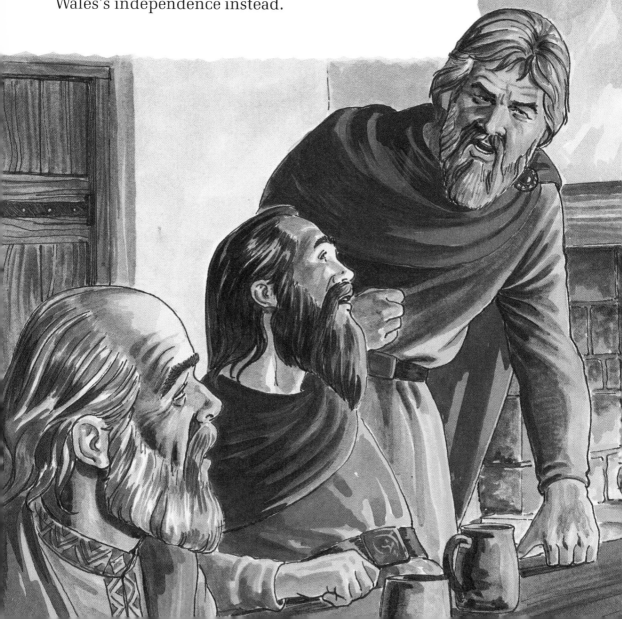

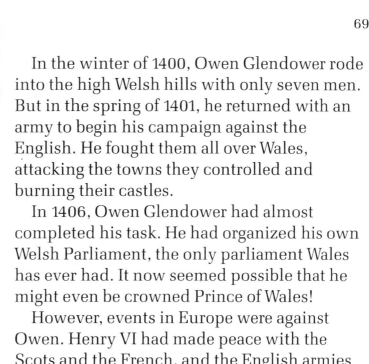

In the winter of 1400, Owen Glendower rode into the high Welsh hills with only seven men. But in the spring of 1401, he returned with an army to begin his campaign against the English. He fought them all over Wales, attacking the towns they controlled and burning their castles.

In 1406, Owen Glendower had almost completed his task. He had organized his own Welsh Parliament, the only parliament Wales has ever had. It now seemed possible that he might even be crowned Prince of Wales!

However, events in Europe were against Owen. Henry VI had made peace with the Scots and the French, and the English armies were now free to deal with the Welsh. By 1407, Owen was in full retreat. His rebellion had finally collapsed.

We don't know what became of Owen Glendower. Perhaps he died in the Welsh hills. Perhaps he managed to escape to another country. He played no further part in ruling Wales which, from that time on, was ruled by the English.

Battle of Bannockburn

Water sprayed into the air as Edward II and his English knights splashed through the shallow stream, called the Bannock burn, on their horses. Then they charged up the hill towards the small Scottish army at the top. As they drew close to the ridge, the leading horses suddenly disappeared from view. The ground seemed to have swallowed them up! Knights crashed to the ground in confusion and the charge broke up in disarray.

The poor animals had tumbled into pits dug by the Scots. From the top of the ridge, the Scottish king, Robert Bruce, waved his army forward. They swept down the slope towards the English, blowing their horns and shouting, "Slay! Slay!" The rest of Edward's knights fled in terror and panic.

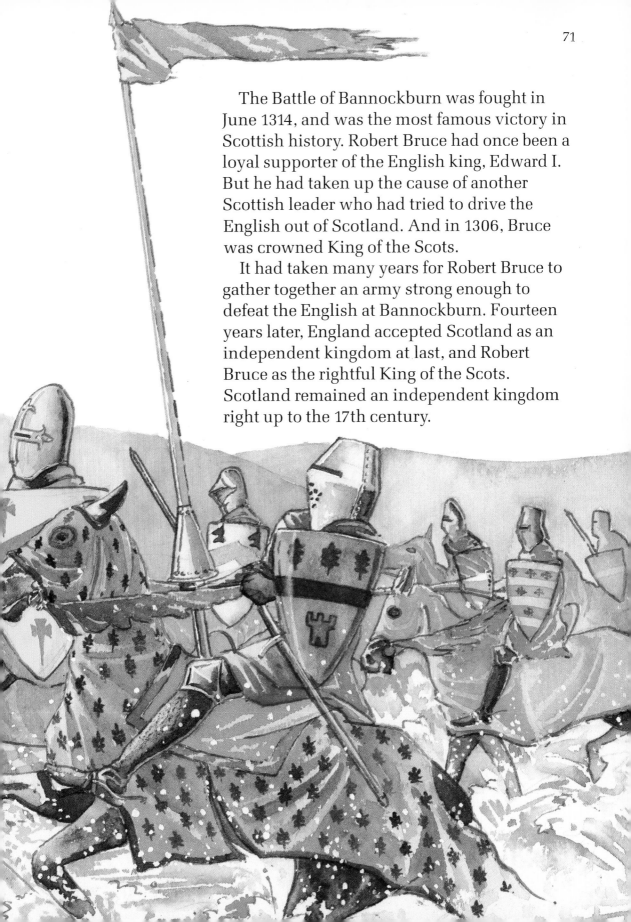

The Battle of Bannockburn was fought in June 1314, and was the most famous victory in Scottish history. Robert Bruce had once been a loyal supporter of the English king, Edward I. But he had taken up the cause of another Scottish leader who had tried to drive the English out of Scotland. And in 1306, Bruce was crowned King of the Scots.

It had taken many years for Robert Bruce to gather together an army strong enough to defeat the English at Bannockburn. Fourteen years later, England accepted Scotland as an independent kingdom at last, and Robert Bruce as the rightful King of the Scots. Scotland remained an independent kingdom right up to the 17th century.

The Hundred Years War

The French cavalry thundered towards the English archers. "Now, fire!" shouted the sergeant. Several thousand bowstrings hummed, and a cloud of arrows curled through the air towards the French cavalry. Then the arrows smashed against their armour, sending knights crashing from their saddles and horses plunging to the ground. The English had won the Battle of Crécy!

This battle was just one of a number which took place during the Hundred Years War. The war lasted from 1337 until 1453. The reasons for it had begun almost three hundred years earlier with William the Conqueror. He had owned lands in France, most of which were lost during the reign of King John. Years later, King Edward III decided to claim all of France back as part of his kingdom.

Edward III marched his army into France. He and his son, the Black Prince, won a number of great victories between them. The Black Prince even managed to take the French king prisoner! But the English still couldn't win the war.

As Edward III grew old, the French began to capture back many of their lost lands. In this war, the advantage seemed to switch from one country to the other until the middle of the 15th century. From then on, the French defeated the English repeatedly and, by 1453, the English had been forced to give up their claims in France. The war was over at last.

The Black Death

Thick smoke billowed from the heap of burning clothes and rolled across the field in a dense cloud. The men coughed as they threw the last of the bodies into the pit. Then, as the empty cart turned and creaked back towards the town, they began wearily to shovel earth over the corpses.

In 1348, a terrible plague arrived in Britain. It was a disease which became known as 'the Black Death'. The clothes and bodies of many of the victims were burned, but the disease still spread rapidly through the dirty, overcrowded towns. Victims of the disease developed boils under their arms, and their bodies were covered with rashes of black spots. Soon they were unable to eat and began to cough blood. After a few days, they died.

Today, scientists call this disease the 'bubonic plague'.

The plague probably started in China and was carried to Britain by black rats living in the holds of ships. Fleas lived on the rats and carried the plague germs to any human beings they bit.

The people of Britain were terrified. They tried everything they could to avoid catching the plague. Many fled into the countryside, often carrying the plague germs with them. But there was no cure. Within a single year, the Black Death had killed about one third of the population of England.

Outbreaks of the plague occurred many times during the next three hundred years, and many villages disappeared for good.

The Peasants' Revolt

The peasants gasped. They couldn't believe their eyes! Their leader, Wat Tyler, had caught hold of the bridle of the king's horse! The Mayor of London, frightened for the king's safety, drew his sword. And as he did so, a fierce mutter of anger swept through the crowd. Tyler had fallen to the ground, dying.

"You have no leader now!" shouted the young king, Richard II, who was only fifteen years old. "Let me be your leader!" He ignored the angry cries of the peasants as he rode towards them. "Go home and I will deal with your problems!" he cried.

Life for the peasants had always been hard, but in 1381, many felt that they had suffered enough. Thousands of peasants, led by Wat Tyler, marched from Kent and Essex towards London.

The peasants wanted to end the old system of working for no pay. They were also angry because heavy taxes had been introduced to pay for the wars against France. They particularly hated the poll tax, now three times its normal level.

On their way to London, the peasants burned down several manor houses. In London, they attacked the houses of the king's ministers and surrounded the Tower of London. Wat Tyler had tried to stop the peasants from looting, but many officials, lawyers and clergy were killed.

After King Richard had spoken to the peasants, they returned home. But their leaders didn't go unpunished. Many of them were killed without trial.

John Wyclif's Bible

In the 14th century, the first English translation of the Bible was made. This was the idea of a man called John Wyclif. It was the first time that the Bible had been written in the language of the ordinary people. Poor travelling preachers, called the Lollards, supported Wyclif's ideas. They used to wander round the countryside, reading the Bible aloud to small crowds of peasants.

Up until the 14th century, the Bible had been written in Latin. Church services were held in Latin too, but the only people who spoke or read Latin were well-educated people or the clergy. Because the ordinary people couldn't understand what was being said, the clergy had great power over them.

Wyclif argued that truth came from God, not from the Pope or the clergy. And he argued that the Church shouldn't interfere in matters which didn't concern it. Wyclif also believed that the clergy had become too powerful. He criticized them for being too rich, and for not leading a pure life.

Wyclif wanted the Church to be reformed, or changed. He also wanted people to read the Bible for themselves.

A hero's welcome!

The church bells pealed as the people cheered and shouted. Small children wriggled to the front of the crowd to catch a glimpse of the king. "Here he comes!" they cried. At last, the royal procession came into view. At the head of the long line of soldiers rode Henry V. The roars of the crowd became deafening as the king passed. It was a hero's welcome!

Henry V returned to England from France in 1415. His army had recently beaten a much larger French force at the Battle of Agincourt, even though food had been in short supply and many of Henry's soldiers had fallen sick. It looked as though the English might win the Hundred Years War!

But the struggle between the two nations dragged on for seven more years. In 1422, Henry died of fever in France. Then the French found a new leader to continue their struggle, a young girl called Joan of Arc. Joan believed she heard voices that came from God. Dressed as a soldier, she led the French army to several victories against the English.

Joan was later captured by the English and burned at the stake as a witch. But by then she had inspired the French people. With the aid of large cannons, they recaptured the cities they had once lost to England. By 1453, they had almost driven the English out of France.

Red Rose, White Rose

The lords fell silent. In the distance, they could hear the clanking of armour as soldiers approached Westminster Hall. Then the doors of the Hall burst open and the nobles and bishops sprang to their feet. For there stood Richard of York. And in front of him walked a man-at-arms, carrying a sharp-edged sword.

Richard strode towards the empty throne and placed his hands firmly on the sword. He was claiming the title, King of England! He turned to face the lords, expecting to hear their shouts of approval. But the lords were silent. They knew that Richard was stealing the throne from his brother, Henry VI.

Henry VI was the rightful King of England, but he was often ill and unable to control the powerful nobles. The leading barons were divided into two groups, the Lancastrians, who supported Henry, and the Yorkists, who supported Richard of York.

War soon broke out. Each side took a rose as its badge. The Yorkists took a white rose and the Lancastrians a red. The war became known as the 'Wars of the Roses'.

But Richard's bold claim to the throne ended badly. Although Parliament declared that Richard could take over as king when Henry died, Richard was too impatient. He fought the Lancastrians at the Battle of Wakefield and was killed.

Henry VI was later declared mad and locked up in the Tower of London. His son, Edward IV, was crowned king. Edward brought peace to the war-torn country but died before he could finish this work. The throne passed to his son who was only a boy of twelve. The Wars of the Roses were still far from over!

The princes in the Tower

Prince Edward hugged his younger brother happily. "I've been so lonely in the Tower by myself," he said. "Now we can have some fun together before my coronation!" The young princes couldn't know that they were both to become victims of the Wars of the Roses.

The twelve-year-old Prince Edward, who took his father's name, and his younger brother, Prince Richard, were the sons of King Edward IV. On his deathbed, the king had named his brother, Richard of Gloucester, as Protector of the Realm. This meant that Richard had to look after Edward's two sons while they were growing up.

Richard of Gloucester sent the princes to stay in the Tower of London. It was quite usual for a future king to stay in the royal apartments before his coronation. But this time, the coronation never took place, and the two young princes were never seen again.

No one actually knows what happened to the boys. According to one story, Richard of Gloucester had them murdered in their beds. Two hundred years later, the bodies of two young boys were found buried in a chest in the Tower. But some experts do not believe they are the bodies of the princes, even though the bones have now been buried in a special tomb in Westminster Abbey.

Perhaps Richard of Gloucester was innocent of the murder. However, he did claim the throne for himself, and in 1483, he was crowned Richard III.

The first Tudor king

The cry rang out across the battlefield, "God save King Henry!" The soldiers cheered as their leader knelt on the blood-stained earth and was crowned king by Lord Stanley.

The new king was Henry VII. He was the first and only king ever to be crowned on a battlefield. It happened on August 22nd 1485, at the end of the Battle of Bosworth. This great battle ended the Wars of the Roses and the reign of Richard III.

Richard was the last king of the Plantagenet family, which had reigned since 1154. Henry came from a new line of rulers called the Tudors, who were a Welsh family.

Henry had been sent to France during the Wars of the Roses, and had seen how unpopular Richard III had become. So he had hired foreign troops and returned to England. Then, with the help of a few powerful English nobles, he had won the crown.

Henry Tudor's claim to the throne wasn't a strong one, so he decided to marry Elizabeth of York. This was a clever plan, because it united the Yorkists and Lancastrians for the first time. Henry joined the White Rose of the Yorkists and the Red Rose of the Lancastrians to make his own badge, the Tudor Rose.

Henry was a good king. He avoided getting involved in expensive wars overseas, and he was careful how he spent the money he raised from taxes. He ruled very carefully, so that even the barons respected him. When he died in 1509, after a reign of twenty-four years, Henry was able to hand on a kingdom which was stronger and richer than ever before.

Wool trade

During the Middle Ages, wool production was the most important industry in Britain. The country's fertile, grassy hills provided excellent grazing for sheep. The raw wool was sold to Flanders, in Belgium, where Flemish weavers wove it into fine cloth.

During the Hundred Years War, many Flemish weavers fled to Britain to set up their looms. They produced their cloth in places like Coventry, Halifax and Norwich. These towns became important centres of the wool industry. Large markets were held there, and cloth was bought and sold.

The fleece was sheared from the sheep.

Merchants bought and sold the cloth. Much of it was sent abroad.

The wool was washed with a special powder.

The wool was combed with metal combs. Then it was spun into thread, which was later woven into cloth on a loom.

The cloth was washed, bleached and dyed.

The printing press

"Your majesty," murmured William Caxton.
"This is a very great honour!" King Edward IV
and the royal family stared at the strange
wooden machine in front of them.

The machine was a printing press. Caxton showed his royal visitors how it worked. Each block of letters was smeared with ink, then pressed onto a sheet of paper. This was repeated again and again until many sheets had been printed, which could then be made into a book. Caxton held out a finished book called 'The Canterbury Tales', written by the famous poet, Geoffrey Chaucer.

Caxton had originally seen the printing press during a visit to Cologne, in Germany. Here, he had visited the workshops of a German called John Gutenberg, who had invented the press. Caxton quickly realized how important printing could be. Books could be produced much more quickly and cheaply on a press than when written by hand.

Caxton started to learn the art of printing. When he returned from Germany to England, he set up his own press near Westminster Abbey, in London. Before he died, he had printed over eighteen thousand pages and produced over one hundred books.

As more printed books appeared, a standard form of written English began to develop. This replaced French and Latin. Up to this time, French had been used by the English aristocracy, and books had been written in Latin by the monks.

Henry VIII

Henry VIII was in a very bad mood. Even the court jester couldn't make him laugh. The royal courtiers kept out of his way and the servants tiptoed nervously about, quietly getting on with their duties.

Henry badly wanted a son. He had become king at the age of eighteen, and had married his brother's widow, Katherine of Aragon. But only one of their children had survived, and she was a girl, called Mary. Henry felt that he could only leave the throne of England in a secure position if he had a son to follow him.

When Katherine became too old to have any more children, Henry decided to divorce her and marry again. So he ordered his chief minister, Cardinal Wolsey, to ask the Pope in Rome to allow the divorce. In 1529, news of the Pope's refusal reached the court.

Henry was furious. Determined to get his own way, he decided that he would have to change the rules of the Church. He declared himself head of the Church in England, instead of the Pope. Now, he was able to divorce Katherine and marry Anne Boleyn, a young lady-in-waiting.

But Anne didn't give Henry a son, either. He soon grew tired of her, and when she was accused of loving another man, he had her executed.

Altogether, Henry married six wives. His third wife, Jane Seymour, finally gave him a son, the future Edward VI. But sadly, she died in childbirth. After Jane came Anne of Cleves, Catherine Howard and Catherine Parr.

Bloody Mary

Mary ruled England
from 1553 to 1558.

The people in the crowd looked at Thomas Cranmer in disbelief. This wasn't what they had come for at all! Their voices began to rise in anger. Then they cried out together, "Away with him!"

The people had gathered in St Mary's Chapel, Oxford, to hear Thomas Cranmer say how sorry he was for supporting the Protestant religion. Now they were angry because he had just made a speech attacking the Pope and the Catholic Church instead. There were furious murmurs as the guards seized Cranmer and marched him away.

Thomas Cranmer had been Archbishop of Canterbury during the reigns of Henry VIII, and the boy-king, Edward VI.

When Edward died, Cranmer had supported Lady Jane Grey's claim to the throne. She was also a Protestant, and her followers didn't want Henry's Catholic daughter, Mary, to become queen.

But Mary seized the throne. She intended to bring back the Catholic faith. Lady Jane Grey and her supporters were executed, and Mary threatened all Protestants with death. Some fled abroad, most changed their religion and a few, like Cranmer, betrayed their religion and signed papers saying they had been wrong.

Then, Cranmer changed his mind about his confession. He was tried and sent to the stake to be burned. He was one of about three hundred Protestants who were executed during Mary's reign. Because of these killings, the queen came to be known as 'Bloody Mary'.

Mary, Queen of Scots

There was a noise of footsteps in the passage. Then the door of the queen's chamber burst open and four men charged into the room.

The four men pulled the trembling David Rizzio from behind the queen's skirts and dragged him away. The door slammed shut and Mary, Queen of Scots, sank to her knees.

The leader of these men was Lord Darnley, Mary's husband. He had become jealous of Rizzio, her Italian secretary. So, helped by a group of Protestants keen to destroy Mary's power, he took him away and murdered him.

From the age of five, Mary, Queen of Scots, had been brought up in the French court. It looked as if she would have wealth, power and happiness as she grew older. But her husband, Francis II of France, had died while he was still young, and Mary had returned to Scotland. She felt very alone because she was a Catholic in a Protestant country.

At that time, Mary's cousin, Elizabeth, was Queen of England. Both women were related to the first Tudor king, Henry VII. So Mary thought that she should become Queen of England, herself, once Elizabeth died.

Soon after Rizzio's death, Lord Darnley was also murdered. Mary then married the man who was accused of killing Darnley. The Scots grew tired of the queen and her plotting, and they rebelled against her. Mary's army was defeated in battle and she fled to England.

In England, Elizabeth was afraid that Mary might overthrow her as queen. So she kept her cousin imprisoned for nineteen years, moving her from one castle to another. Mary still plotted against Elizabeth, however. And in 1587, Elizabeth signed Mary's death warrant.

Royal progresses

Queen Elizabeth I clapped her hands with delight as the barge moved smoothly across the lake towards her. It was covered with flowers and towed by fabulous sea creatures. Mermaids swam in the water around it. Watching the scene, the Earl of Hertford sighed with relief. The royal visit to his house at Elvetham was going to be a success!

Every summer, Queen Elizabeth would tour the country with members of her court. They would stay in the houses of the richest lords and earls in the kingdom. These hosts would arrange balls, banquets, pageants and plays to amuse the Queen.

The tours were called royal 'progresses'. Hundreds of pack-horses and carts would carry the belongings of Elizabeth and her courtiers, and thousands of cheering people would line the roads to watch her pass. In every town she visited, the mayor and the council would welcome her with presents.

By travelling around in this way, Elizabeth saw her kingdom, and the people saw their queen. The progresses helped Elizabeth to win the love and affection of her subjects.

Elizabeth had a number of favourite male courtiers, but she never married. She reigned for forty-five years. When she died in 1603, she had no children to follow her, so her chief ministers offered the throne to James VI of Scotland.

A play at the Globe

The boy and his father hurried towards the Globe Theatre. They had pushed their way through the jostling crowds on London Bridge and now they could see the flag flying from the roof of the theatre.

Once inside, they took their places on the level ground in front of the stage. The boy looked around at the wealthy people who sat in the balconies under the roof. In front of them, noisy crowds of apprentices chatted to one another, enjoying an afternoon off work. Then they heard the sound of the trumpet, the signal for the play to begin!

For centuries, groups of travelling actors had been performing religious plays. These usually took place in inn yards. The Globe Theatre was one of the first theatres to be built. It had its own company of actors.

The Globe was placed outside the walls of London, so that the huge crowds who flocked there couldn't cause trouble inside the city. Audiences in the 16th century were much noisier than audiences today! They laughed and argued during the play, and shouted for ale and tobacco.

Most of the plays performed at the Globe were written by William Shakespeare. He didn't use stories from the Bible, like many playwrights before him. He wrote history plays, comedies and tragedies, as well as stories of love, war, treachery and power.

Shakespeare wrote some of the wittiest and some of the most moving plays in the English language. Today, his plays are performed all over the world, and are as well loved as ever.

The Spanish Armada

The cabin boy stared across the glistening water at the huge Spanish warships. He felt very alarmed. They were great ships with tall sides, and each one had a towering stern which rose high above the water.

As the boy watched, smoke filled the air above the grey sea. The air seemed to crack and whine as cannon-balls flew, and the boy could hear the noise of splintering wood. He prayed for the battle to be over.

The year was 1588. The Spanish king had sent a huge armada, or fleet of ships, from Spain to conquer England. The Armada was made up of twenty warships, called galleons, and forty-four merchant ships which had been turned into warships.

The English knew in advance that the Armada was coming and they sailed out to meet it. Their galleons were smaller, lower and faster than the Spanish ships, and they could move around better. Although the Spanish had drawn up a plan of battle, the English were well prepared. They attacked as the Armada sailed up the English Channel.

The attack lasted six days. Then the Spanish ships sailed into the harbour at Calais, in France. The English sent blazing fire-ships after them to force them out, and the Spaniards panicked. Finally, a storm drove the scattered vessels of the Armada northwards and many were sunk. Some were blown ashore in Ireland. Of the 130 ships that had set sail, only 67 returned to Spain.

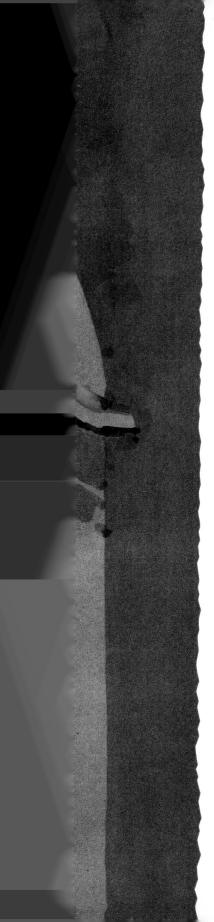

The gunpowder plot

It was midnight. In the doorway which led to the cellars of Parliament House, there lurked a shadowy figure. He had wrapped a cloak closely around him and was shivering with cold. He had come to carry out a task.

Suddenly, the man spun round. He had heard a loud clatter of boots on the cobbles behind as guards appeared out of the gloom. Their leader shouted out, "Arrest that man! Search the cellar!"

The evening was November 5th 1605, and the man was Guy Fawkes. He had planned to blow up Parliament, killing the king, queen, lords, bishops and Members of Parliament, who were all in the building at the time. In the cellar underneath Parliament House, the guards found thirty-six barrels of gunpowder hidden under a heap of coal and logs. Guy Fawkes was carrying three matches, a slow fuse and a watch.

The plot had been planned by a group of Catholic gentlemen led by Sir Robert Catesby. The Protestant Queen Elizabeth had died in 1603, and the Catholic James I had become king. English Catholics now hoped to be allowed to worship in their own churches. They also wanted an end to the torture and execution of Catholic priests.

But James decided to banish Catholic priests, and to fine everyone who practised the Catholic faith. Guy Fawkes might have succeeded in his task but for one of his fellow plotters who betrayed him. Although no one was hurt, the king's chief minister, Sir Robert Cecil, had all the plotters executed.

Civil War

The pikemen of the New Model Army levelled their long weapons through the splutter of musket-fire. They presented a wall of razor-sharp points to the Royalist soldiers who advanced steadily towards them. Then a trumpet call echoed across the field and the cavalry of the New Model Army crashed into the enemy. Within minutes, the Royalist soldiers had fled in confusion.

The year was 1645. Cromwell's army had just defeated the Royalists at the Battle of Naseby. The Royalists were supporters of Charles I, who was crowned king in 1625. During his reign, Charles had quarrelled with Parliament over almost everything, including religion and money.

Charles had eventually decided to rule the country without Parliament. He raised heavy taxes, which people disliked, and he even tried to change the religious ceremonies and beliefs of the English and Scottish churches.

Then, in 1639, the Scottish army had invaded England. Charles was forced to call Parliament, because he needed money from them. But the Members of Parliament were determined to reduce the king's power, so they demanded changes in government. The quarrel developed into full-scale civil war.

Oliver Cromwell realized that Parliament could never win the war without a properly-trained army. So he formed the New Model Army. This consisted of well-trained men who believed strongly that they were right. This army defeated the Royalists at the Battle of Naseby. King Charles was captured, imprisoned, and later tried for treason. In 1649, he was beheaded.

Lord Protector

Oliver Cromwell was furious. He was Captain-General of the army, the most powerful man in the country, yet Parliament refused to do what he wanted!

Ever since the execution of Charles I, four years before, Cromwell had expected a new Parliament to take the place of the old one. But he had just heard that the Members of Parliament were again failing to do what they had promised.

So, in 1653, Cromwell got rid of Parliament. He summoned his guards and burst into the Chamber of Parliament, crying, "Begone, you rogues!" The Members of Parliament were pushed out roughly as he added, "You have sat here long enough!"

Cromwell then began to rule the country himself. He didn't call himself king but used the title 'Lord Protector of England' instead.

As Lord Protector, Cromwell was influenced by a religious group called the Puritans. These people believed in hard work, and in a simple, religious life. They disapproved of pleasures and entertainments. It was the Puritans who persuaded Cromwell to pass new laws banning the celebration of Christmas and Easter. People were fined for working on Sundays. Maypoles were cut down and alehouses closed.

Cromwell was successful in winning wars overseas, and he allowed people to worship more freely. But many people disliked his Puritan ideals. So when Cromwell died in 1658, a great many Englishmen were ready to see a king in control of their country again.

Fire and plague

The sky was lit by a strange orange glow as flames roared through the closely-packed, wooden houses. A dense cloud of black smoke billowed over the city. London was on fire!

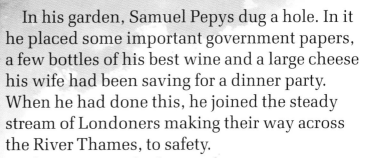

In his garden, Samuel Pepys dug a hole. In it he placed some important government papers, a few bottles of his best wine and a large cheese his wife had been saving for a dinner party. When he had done this, he joined the steady stream of Londoners making their way across the River Thames, to safety.

The Great Fire had started in 1666, in a baker's shop in Pudding Lane. Fanned by a strong wind, the fire burned for two days. It destroyed thousands of houses, as well as London Bridge, the old St Paul's Cathedral and over a hundred other churches.

The Great Fire was a terrible disaster, but it did some good as well. In 1665, plague had swept through the city. The disease had spread rapidly through the filthy narrow streets and courtyards, killing thousands of people. The fire at least destroyed the slums where the plague germs could breed.

Now the city could be rebuilt. The architect, Sir Christopher Wren, turned London into a beautiful city. He designed fine, wide streets with houses made of brick and stone, and many fine churches. His masterpiece is St Paul's Cathedral, which still stands today.

Samuel Pepys kept a diary which tells us a great deal about this period of history. A few days after the Great Fire, he wrote that he returned to his garden and that the papers and the wine were quite safe. He forgot to mention whether the cheese had survived!

The Glorious Revolution

A mysterious barge moved slowly down the River Thames. As it slid through the calm water, a figure stood up. He dropped an object overboard and watched it sink from sight.

This object was the Great Seal of England, used to mark official documents agreed to by the king. The figure was King James II, who was leaving Britain never to return. He hoped that his enemies would find it hard to govern the country without the Great Seal.

James was fleeing to France. He was a Catholic. He had been a popular king at the beginning of his reign, but his enemies wanted their next monarch to be a Protestant. James had two daughters, both of them Protestants. Then, in 1688, everything changed. James II had a son!

The Protestant nobles realized that the boy would be brought up a Catholic. And this meant that a whole line of Catholic kings might follow! So they invited William of Orange to come to England to save the Protestant faith. William of Orange was the Protestant Dutch ruler, and the husband of James' elder daughter, Mary.

William landed at Torbay with an army of fifteen thousand men. James lost his nerve when some of his generals abandoned him, and fled to France. The Members of Parliament declared that, by fleeing, James had given up his throne. They made William and Mary joint rulers of England. We call this period the Glorious Revolution.

Queen Anne's reign

The Duke's horse moved about restlessly, stamping the ground with impatience. The Duke scribbled a note to his wife on the back of a tavern bill. Then, folding it in two, he handed it to an officer, who turned and galloped off at great speed towards England.

This note contained the first news of the Duke of Marlborough's great victory at the Battle of Blenheim in 1704. The battle had been fought on the River Danube to save Vienna, in Austria, from the army of Louis XIV, the King of France. Dutch, German and Austrian forces had helped Britain win. But the victory still showed that Britain had become a great European power.

Back in England, Queen Anne, who ruled England after William and Mary, presented the Duke of Marlborough with a magnificent palace near Oxford. This gift was given to thank the duke for the victory. It was named Blenheim Palace, in honour of the battle.

In 1713, the long war against France finally ended. Britain now controlled many lands abroad. And the government was richer than ever before. It could borrow large sums of money from wealthy merchants through the Bank of England. This bank had been set up during the reign of William and Mary.

Art and science flourished during Queen Anne's reign. And many of the things we are familiar with today came into daily use. For example, there were newpapers, banks, coffee houses, spectacles and even umbrellas!

The landowners

The walls of the last house crashed to the
ground, and the workmen began to load the
rubble onto a cart. The duke nodded with
satisfaction. As soon as the village had been
demolished, he could start building his new
gardens at Chatsworth.

   In the 18th century, it was fashionable for
landowners to create spectacular gardens.
Everything was done on a grand scale. Woods
were planted. Lakes, fountains, and waterfalls
were introduced. Temples and bridges were
built. Like many others, the Duke of
Devonshire wanted a garden designed by the
landscape gardener, Capability Brown. And if
a village was in the way, then he would move
the whole thing out of sight!

Landowning families, like the Devonshires, had great power in Britain during the 18th century. Most landowners sat in the House of Lords, and many served in the king's government. All of them controlled the lives of the people who lived on their estates. They often took their position very seriously, trying out new farming methods to improve the land.

For example, Lord Townshend showed that turnips both improved the soil and provided useful winter fodder for animals.

These great landed families held great banquets, led the local hunt, and presided over the local courts of law. They became the centre of life in the countryside.

The Bow Street Runners

"I arrest you in the name of the king!" The door crashed open and the robbers leaped to their feet in horror. John Townshend and five Bow Street Runners burst into the room with their pistols cocked.

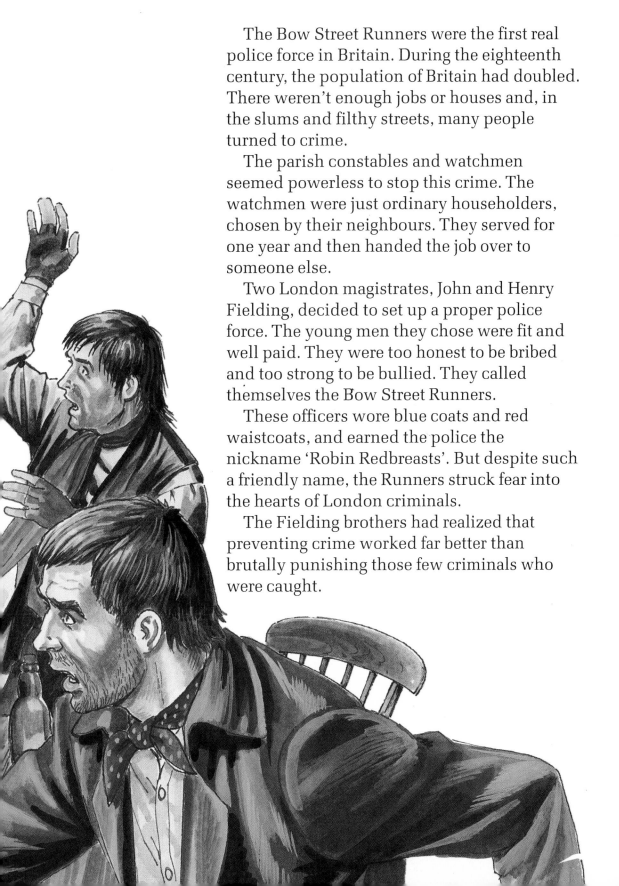

The Bow Street Runners were the first real police force in Britain. During the eighteenth century, the population of Britain had doubled. There weren't enough jobs or houses and, in the slums and filthy streets, many people turned to crime.

The parish constables and watchmen seemed powerless to stop this crime. The watchmen were just ordinary householders, chosen by their neighbours. They served for one year and then handed the job over to someone else.

Two London magistrates, John and Henry Fielding, decided to set up a proper police force. The young men they chose were fit and well paid. They were too honest to be bribed and too strong to be bullied. They called themselves the Bow Street Runners.

These officers wore blue coats and red waistcoats, and earned the police the nickname 'Robin Redbreasts'. But despite such a friendly name, the Runners struck fear into the hearts of London criminals.

The Fielding brothers had realized that preventing crime worked far better than brutally punishing those few criminals who were caught.

Visiting the spas

During the eighteenth century, the wealthiest people often travelled to special centres throughout England. Here, they would take, or drink, the waters that bubbled up from hot springs in the earth. The water from these springs was rich in minerals which people believed would keep them healthy and cure many illnesses.

Towns eventually grew up around the springs. These towns, such as Bath and Tunbridge Wells, were called 'spa' towns. The name came from a town called Spa in Belgium, which was famous for its hot springs.

Bath, a city in the south-west of England, was one of the favourite spa towns. Whole families used to arrive in the city by stage-coach, and sometimes they stayed for several months. The older people would usually come to Bath for a rest, while younger visitors came to enjoy the balls and evening parties, or perhaps to find a husband or wife.

At the time, the Master of Ceremonies in Bath was Beau Nash, a man famous for his white-feathered hats and white waistcoats. He helped to organize the many events in the town. He controlled the gambling tables and made up the rules for the balls, assemblies and concerts.

It was largely because of Beau Nash that Bath became such a fashionable city to visit. Later, Jane Austen, the novelist, wrote about Bath in her novels. The characters she created came from the society people who visited the spa. Her books are very witty and amusing.

Battle of Culloden

The mist swept across Culloden Moor and the Scottish clansmen shivered. They had only eaten one biscuit each the day before, and now they were hungry and exhausted. The roar of the English cannon could be heard thundering above the mournful sound of the Scottish bagpipes.

The clansmen needed more than sheer bravery or sharp Scottish swords to win against the English, for the English cannon fired small balls, called grapeshot. This mowed the clansmen down and drove their leader, Bonnie Prince Charlie, from the battlefield.

Bonnie Prince Charlie's real name was Charles Stuart and his followers were called Jacobites. When he landed in Scotland, in August 1745, many of the Scottish clans had gathered together to join him.

As the Jacobites advanced south, the people of London panicked. But Bonnie Prince Charlie's army was too small to attack the capital, and at Derby he was advised to turn back. He got as far as Culloden before the English army of well-trained Redcoats, who were hard on his heels, forced his army to face them in battle. The Jacobites were defeated.

Bonnie Prince Charlie escaped to France, helped by loyal Highlanders like Flora MacDonald. The Duke of Cumberland, who led the Redcoats, had all the wounded Scots killed on the battlefield. Because of this, he came to be known as 'the Butcher'. He drove out Bonnie Prince Charlie's supporters, seized their lands, and sent many thousands as prisoners to the West Indies.

So ended Charles Stuart's disastrous attempt to overthrow the king, George II, and to restore the Stuart family to the British throne.

Britain loses America

"Here come the lobsters!" shouted an American, as he spotted the red uniforms of the British army. His fellow soldiers, in their worn buckskins and fringed hunting shirts, grinned at one another.

The line of British Redcoats came to a halt and laid down their muskets. Then their commander, General Cornwallis, surrendered to the American general, George Washington. The American War of Independence had finally come to an end.

The surrender of the British army took place at Yorktown in 1781. The war had started because the thirteen American colonies had grown tired of paying heavy taxes to Britain. The Americans had no proper army, and few people thought they could win. But the tough American farmers were well able to stand up to the British soldiers.

The Americans also received help from the French, who wanted revenge for all the times they had been defeated by the British in India and Canada. And the British government found it hard to organize a war which was being fought thousands of miles away. Supplies took months to reach America.

The war wasn't popular among the British people, either. Many felt that the Americans were right in fighting for their freedom, just as the Britons had done throughout their history. After the loss of America, one British statesman said, "If England is free, and America is free, the whole world can never be slaves." Many people felt the same way.

Life in the factories

The little girl was so tired she could hardly keep her eyes open. Stumbling in between the clanking spinning-machines, she staggered under the weight of the heavy bobbins. She put down her load for a moment to breathe.

As she stood there, the overseer swung his stick at her. "Get moving!" he roared.

This little girl worked in one of the new cloth factories of northern England. Before the 1750s, all the spinning and weaving had been done in the homes of the country workers. But important changes were now taking place. Large, water-powered machines had been invented to spin and weave cotton, and these were later replaced by machines powered by steam. This meant that cloth had to be produced in factories in the towns.

When the factories first started, there were no rules to govern safety, and no laws to say how many hours each man, woman or child must work. There were also thousands of child-workers. A child of eleven might be expected to work for fourteen hours a day! Poor families often had to send their children out to work, in order to make enough money to live on.

Accidents in the factories were common. Often, exhausted children would fall against unguarded machinery. Some factory owners looked after their workers, but there were many who did not. They would pay low wages and expect long hours of work. And some overseers were very cruel.

Then, in 1833, proper factory laws were introduced into Britain. In the 1840s, a Member of Parliament called Lord Shaftesbury told people about the problems. He helped to improve factory conditions and, because he worked so hard to help children, he became known as 'the children's friend'.

War with France

The gun crew crowded round the cannon. Its barrel was still hot from firing. The crew quickly sponged it down with cold water and reloaded with a fresh cartridge and cannon-ball. Then they threw all their weight against the ropes, and the gun rumbled into place.

"Fire!" yelled the gunner. There was an almighty crash as the cannon rolled back and smoke swirled through the low gun deck. They had hit the target! They cheered as the masts of the French ship toppled and fell.

The British navy was fighting a sea battle against France in a war which lasted from 1793 until 1815. In 1789, there had been a revolution in France. The king, Louis XVI, had been executed, and various groups had struggled to seize power. During this chaotic period, a new leader emerged called Napoleon Bonaparte. In time, Napoleon became Emperor of France, but his real ambition was to become master of all Europe.

The British government decided to stop Napoleon's plans, so they sent British forces to fight the French. In 1805, the powerful British navy won a great victory against the French and Spanish fleets at the Battle of Trafalgar. The navy was led by Admiral Lord Nelson. When Nelson was killed at Trafalgar, the whole of Britain mourned.

Although British forces controlled the seas, they had to defeat Napoleon's troops on land, too. So the British army was made larger. It won victories in Spain and Portugal and then, under the Duke of Wellington, it defeated Napoleon's army at the Battle of Waterloo in 1815. Napoleon was imprisoned on the Isle of St Helena, where he died in 1821.

The Peterloo Massacre

The mounted soldiers flashed their swords in the air and spurred their horses into the mass of screaming people. Banners bearing the words 'The Rights of Man' were trampled underfoot. Men, women and children tried to escape the hooves of the charging animals.

Within a few minutes, the field in which sixty thousand people had gathered a short while before, was almost empty. Those who remained were lying on the ground, either dead or seriously injured.

It was August 1819. Thousands of citizens had gathered in St Peter's Field, in Manchester, to hear a famous speaker called Orator Hunt. Hunt wanted to change the rules about voting so that MPs could be elected by everyone. Up until then, only people who owned property could vote.

After Britain had defeated Napoleon at Waterloo in 1815, many people were unable to find work. In many factories, skilled workers were replaced by machines. The price of bread had become very high. The poor couldn't afford to buy food, yet they could be hanged for either stealing food or poaching.

Riots became common, and the government put these down ruthlessly. At Peterloo, the Manchester magistrates were afraid that such a large crowd of people might threaten law and order. So they sent local, part-time soldiers to arrest Hunt. But the soldiers were nervous and afraid. They panicked and attacked the crowd. Eleven people died and four hundred were injured. The incident became known as the 'Peterloo Massacre'.

Railway travel

The judges checked their watches and gave the signal. Smoke started to billow from the funnel of the engine. Then the crowds cheered wildly as the 'Rocket' gathered speed and thundered down the track.

It was 1829, and the engine was taking part in a competition held at Rainhill, near Liverpool. The judges were looking for the fastest and most reliable steam locomotive to pull trucks and carriages along the new railway line from Liverpool to Manchester.

The owner of the winning entry was George Stephenson. His engine, the 'Rocket', travelled at the amazing speed of forty-eight kilometres per hour! Just one year after the competition, the railway line was opened. It had been built so that raw cotton could be moved from the port of Liverpool to the cloth factories of Manchester. But soon the railway was also carrying over a thousand passengers every day.

A new age of railway travel had begun. In the years that followed, hundreds of railways were built. They created thousands of new jobs for people and changed life in Britain. They provided the first fast and reliable way for carrying the letters and parcels of the Royal Mail service.

More people could now afford to make trips to the seaside. Fresh fish, vegetables and dairy goods were quickly transported to all parts of the country.

Chartists unite!

A huge crowd of protesters moved slowly along the south bank of the River Thames. It was heading for the Houses of Parliament. But in front of the protesters stood a thin line of soldiers. A murmur ran through the crowd. Some of the marchers could see cannons positioned threateningly on river barges nearby. Their enthusiasm fell. The rain only made things worse.

Then the protesters raised a cheer. Their leader, Feargus O'Connor, was driving off towards Downing Street to deliver their petition to the Prime Minister.

These protesters were known as 'Chartists' after the charters, or petitions, which they wrote. Most of the Chartists were working men. They hoped that by presenting the government with lists of their demands, each signed by millions of people, they could improve living conditions for themselves.

In 1848, only one man out of seven, and no woman, was allowed to vote. Elections were held in the open air where voters could be bullied into voting in a particular way. The Chartists wanted to change Parliament and the way the Members were elected.

But when the charters were examined, signatures were found which were obviously forged. As a result, the Chartists lost faith in their leaders and turned to other movements. Then, as economic conditions improved in England, Chartist activity came to an end. Many of the Chartist ideas were taken up by later governments.

A band of nurses

Florence Nightingale moved quietly in between the rows of beds like a ghost. Her tiny, flickering lamp lit up the grim, dark ward which was packed with wounded soldiers. They lay on straw mattresses, groaning with pain or fever.

Every few paces, Florence Nightingale paused to whisper a word of comfort or encouragement to one of them, or to place a cool hand on a hot forehead. Many of the soldiers were so unused to such gentle treatment that they wept. Some even kissed her shadow as it passed.

Florence was the child of rich parents. When they discovered that their daughter wanted to be a nurse, they were very shocked. For in the 19th century, nurses were untrained and badly paid.

Florence Nightingale was determined to change the nursing situation. In 1854, she offered to nurse soldiers in the Crimean War, in Turkey. Despite the suspicion of many of the doctors, she and her small band of nurses had soon transformed the filthy wards. Florence came to be known as 'the lady with the lamp'.

When Florence returned to Britain, she started the Nightingale School for Nurses in London. There she trained nurses carefully, always insisting on high standards of cleanliness and behaviour.

Throughout the 19th century, medical treatments improved. Doctors started to use anaesthetics to deaden pain during operations. They used antiseptics to stop the spread of infection. And chloroform was used to reduce the pain of women in childbirth.

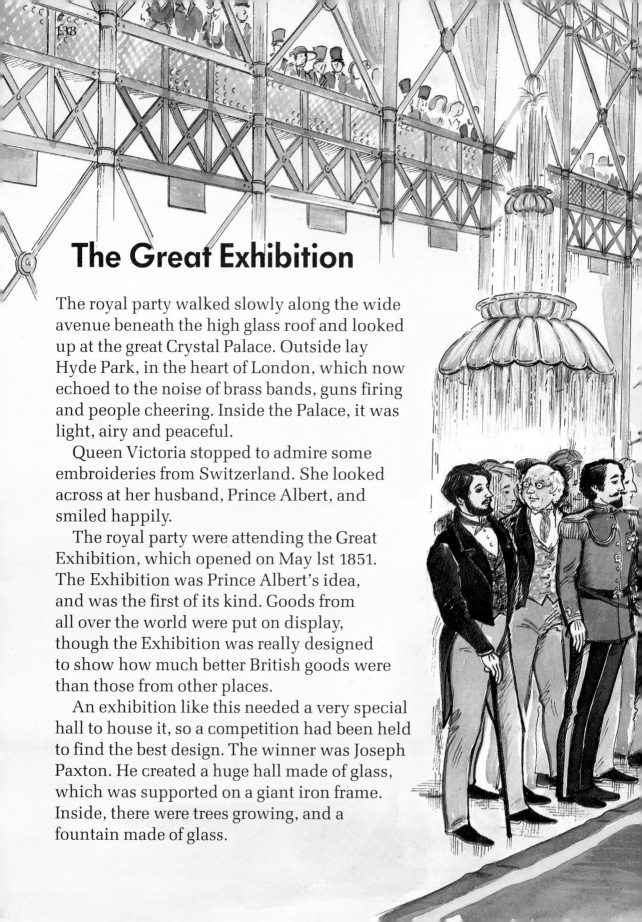

The Great Exhibition

The royal party walked slowly along the wide
avenue beneath the high glass roof and looked
up at the great Crystal Palace. Outside lay
Hyde Park, in the heart of London, which now
echoed to the noise of brass bands, guns firing
and people cheering. Inside the Palace, it was
light, airy and peaceful.

Queen Victoria stopped to admire some
embroideries from Switzerland. She looked
across at her husband, Prince Albert, and
smiled happily.

The royal party were attending the Great
Exhibition, which opened on May 1st 1851.
The Exhibition was Prince Albert's idea,
and was the first of its kind. Goods from
all over the world were put on display,
though the Exhibition was really designed
to show how much better British goods were
than those from other places.

An exhibition like this needed a very special
hall to house it, so a competition had been held
to find the best design. The winner was Joseph
Paxton. He created a huge hall made of glass,
which was supported on a giant iron frame.
Inside, there were trees growing, and a
fountain made of glass.

Over six million people came to visit the Palace. Many travelled by train on special cheap tours arranged by a travel agent. The profits from the Exhibition went towards the building of the Victoria and Albert Museum.

Votes for women!

The horses came round the curve at full gallop! All eyes were on the leading riders.

No one noticed a young woman duck under the safety rail on one side of the track.

Then, as the horses thundered towards her, she stepped out and threw herself under the king's horse. The crowd shouted out. Their roars of excitement turned to gasps of horror as they watched the terrible scene!

The year was 1913, and the race was the Derby at Epsom. The young woman who was killed was a 'suffragette' called Emily Davison. The suffragettes were a group of women determined to win 'suffrage', meaning to be allowed to vote. Two women, Emily and Christobel Pankhurst, had started the movement, holding demonstrations and rallies in the open air outside Parliament.

When the government took no notice of the suffragettes, they became violent. They smashed shop windows, chained themselves to railings, set fire to pillar boxes and cut telegraph wires. Many were arrested and sent to prison. There, they continued to protest by going on hunger strike.

In spite of these protests, the Members of Parliament, who were all men, argued that women weren't fit to vote. In fact, they argued that the women's violent behaviour proved it!

In 1918, a new law allowed men to vote at twenty-one, while women had to wait until they were thirty! It would be another ten years before women over twenty-one would be allowed to vote.

Britain at war

The heavy guns fell silent and an eerie peace descended upon the battlefield. In the trenches, the soldiers crouched out of sight.

At last they heard the sound of a shrill whistle which meant they had to clamber out of the trenches. Stumbling under the weight of their heavy packs, with their bayonets at the ready, the soldiers moved towards the enemy lines.

These soldiers were fighting in the First World War. The war began in 1914, when Germany declared war on Russia. Within days, Britain, France and the country known as Austria-Hungary had joined the conflict.

This war was unlike any earlier European war. The enemy were heavily defended by machine-guns and barbed wire. It was almost impossible to break through. The armies on both sides had to burrow through trenches in the ground for safety.

Lines of these trenches stretched from Switzerland to the English Channel. Heavy guns pounded the enemy on both sides, and villages and forests were destroyed. The land between the trenches became a wasteland of bombshell holes and bodies.

The casualties were terrible. On a single summer's day in 1916, at the Battle of the Somme, sixty thousand British soldiers were killed or injured in one morning.

At last, in 1918, the war ended. Britain, France and the USA had won. The USA had joined the fight in 1917. But victory was achieved at a terrible price. Many thousands of young men had lost their lives.

Life between the wars

The men marched in a long line through the rain. People on the pavement clapped as they went past and handed them sandwiches and mugs of tea. Two of the men held up a banner which flapped in the wind. On it was written the 'Jarrow Crusade'.

The Jarrow Crusade took place in 1936. The men marched from Jarrow, in the north-east of England, to London in the south.

Most of the men had worked in Palmer's shipyard. When this closed, they lost their jobs. There were no other jobs in the area, so the unemployed shipworkers were forced to ask for a weekly payment, or 'dole', from the government. Life on the dole was hard. The money was only just enough to live on.

The Jarrow marchers wanted to draw attention to the troubles of the unemployed. They hoped that by walking four hundred and fifty kilometres to London, they would get more help from the government. But the government ministers told the marchers that there was nothing they could do for them.

Life wasn't so hard in other parts of the country. In the Midlands and the south, new industries were springing up. Men worked in factories which produced motor cars and electrical goods.

New, man-made materials, such as rayon and nylon, were introduced, and these changed the look of women's clothing. Electricity provided power, light and heat, and made various forms of entertainment possible, such as the cinema.

The men on the Jarrow Crusade marched all the way from Jarrow to London. They wanted to draw the attention of government ministers to the troubles of unemployed workers.

The Blitz

The wail of the air-raid siren woke the young woman. She wrapped some blankets around her sleepy children and hurried them into the garden. They clambered down the steps into the bomb shelter and sat, huddled together, listening to the distant thud of falling bombs.

When the all-clear had sounded, the family climbed out of the shelter and stood outside, watching the distant flames of burning buildings light up the night sky.

During the Blitz, in 1940, thousands of German aeroplanes dropped bombs onto British cities. Many of these were fire, or 'incendiary', bombs. People built bomb shelters in their gardens and, in London, many people slept in underground stations for safety. But thousands of people were killed, and many others lost their homes.

The Civil Defence teams and the Royal Air Force fought back as hard as they could, and eventually the German attacks became less frequent. Finally, they ended. The Battle of Britain had been won.

The Second World War lasted from 1939 to 1945. Despite the damage and destruction it caused, it did bring a few benefits to people as well. Among these were new opportunities for women. Many women were able to join the armed forces, and others worked on farms and in weapons factories. The government provided better medical care, and the health of the people improved.

Everyone hoped that these changes would continue after the war was over, and bring a better quality of life for all.

a television

an electric kettle

a washing-machine

a non-stick frying-pan

Britain recovers

When the Second World War ended, many people believed that everything would change for the better. Changes did come, but they came slowly. For instance, some food had been rationed during the war. This meant that there was a limit to how much food each family was allowed. Rationing continued right up until the end of the 1940s.

During the 1950s, the British people worked hard to recover from the destruction caused by the war. New homes were built. These replaced houses in the cities that had been destroyed by the bombing. They also replaced some of the old slums. And local councils built inexpensive houses and rented them out to people at a cheap rate.

Council houses were fitted with modern kitchens and bathrooms. Many of them were also supplied with new gadgets, such as televisions, electric kettles, washing-machines and non-stick frying-pans.

Education improved. New schools and universities were built. Children could now have a much better education than their parents had ever known.

Money would be raised on 'flag days' to pay for equipment and machines in the hospitals. People would sell tiny paper flags to be worn on jackets and coats. But, in 1948, the government introduced the National Health Service. Now, doctors and medical supplies were paid for out of taxes. Visits to the doctor, medicine and hospital treatment were free for everyone.

Sport in Britain

A great roar erupted from Wembley Stadium as England's captain, Bobby Moore, held up the World Cup to show the crowd. England had beaten West Germany in the final and had won the greatest prize in international soccer!

Many of the games played today were invented in Britain. Soccer is the most popular team sport in the world. Its rules were laid down in Victorian times. For over a hundred years, Britain has produced many famous players, such as Stanley Matthews, Bobby Charlton and George Best. And clubs like Manchester United, Liverpool and Spurs have fan clubs all over the world.

Cricket is another British team sport played in many parts of the world. Great cricketers like Jack Hobbs, Len Hutton and Ian Botham have thrilled spectators in test matches.

Ian Botham is a great all-round cricketer.

England won the World Cup in 1966.

Gareth Edwards scores a try in rugby for Wales.

Virginia Wade won Wimbledon in 1977.

Rugby football is a famous Victorian sport. Many fine players have come from the Welsh valleys, such as Barry John, Gareth Edwards and J.P.R. Williams. The game of Rugby has produced a British team called the Lions.

The greatest of the international tennis tournaments is Wimbledon. This is held in London every year and is played on grass courts. Tennis was first played in the early 16th century and, even today, a very early tennis court can still be seen at Hampton Court Palace, near London. Britain's most famous Wimbledon champions were Fred Perry, Ann Jones and, most recently, Virginia Wade, who won in 1977.

Britain is also famous for its amateur sportsplayers. The dedication of athletes like Sebastian Coe, Mary Rand and Daley Thompson has led to some thrilling gold medal performances at the Olympic Games.

Golf has also given Britain some sporting heroes. Tony Jacklin and Nick Faldo are two great golfing champions.

Sebastian Coe is a great middle-distance runner.

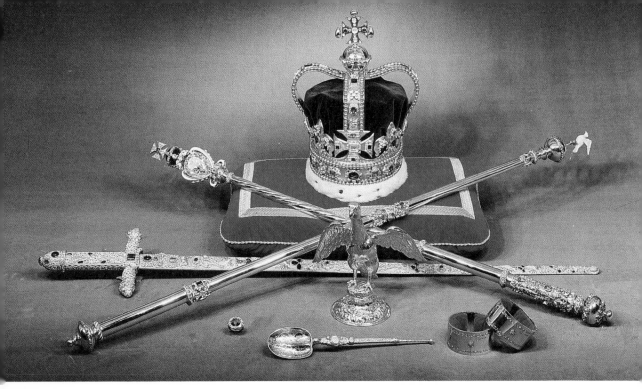

Visitors are amazed by the Crown Jewels.

A visit to Britain

St Paul's Cathedral was built by Christopher Wren.

Every year, crowds of visitors arrive in Britain to visit places of historic interest. Many people go to the Tower of London to see the Crown Jewels. In the Tower, Lady Jane Grey was imprisoned before her execution. So were two of Henry VIII's wives. And the sons of Edward IV may have been murdered there by Richard of Gloucester. Prisoners used to be taken up the River Thames by boat, and would enter the Tower through Traitor's Gate.

There are many other historic monuments to see in London — St Paul's Cathedral, built by Christopher Wren, Nelson's monument in Trafalgar Square, and the London home of the royal family, Buckingham Palace.

In other parts of Britain, places of interest include 18th-century gardens, Norman castles, 12th-century cathedrals, and ancient monuments like the remains of Offa's Dyke.

But Britain isn't just one huge museum. As a modern city, London houses St Katherine Docks, which are now homes for the wealthy, and the International Stock Exchange in the City of London, which is a centre of international banking. The Channel Tunnel site will connect Britain to Europe for the first time, by rail, and Heathrow Airport is the busiest international airport in the world.

Britain has become an important nation by selling its products abroad. It is a small island, but it is a fascinating country to visit.

Heathrow is a busy international airport.

Old docklands are being turned into luxury homes.

Special words

Black Death   A disease which we know today as the 'bubonic plague'.

Chartists   Protesters who wrote their complaints on petitions, or charters.

Crusade   A war of the 'Cross', or a Christian Holy War.

Danegeld   A tax imposed upon the people of England. The money raised from this tax was used to bribe Viking raiders into leaving the country.

Danelaw   The name given to the Viking half of Britain after Alfred's victory over the Vikings. It included the modern counties of Yorkshire, Lincolnshire, Leicestershire and much of East Anglia.

Iceni   One of the Celtic tribes of Britain. Boudicca was an Iceni queen.

Jacobites   Followers of Charles Stuart who wanted to restore the Stuart family to the throne of England during the reign of George II.

joust   A mock battle fought between two knights on horseback. Jousts were a form of practice battle when knights were not at war.

Lollards   Travelling preachers who supported the ideas of John Wyclif.

Lammas   A harvest festival held on August 1st during the Middle Ages.

manor   An estate or area of land granted by barons to their knights.

march   A border area. The Welsh marches included the borderland between England and Wales.

melée	A kind of joust in which many knights fought at the same time.
Muslim	A follower of Islam. Islam is the religion founded by the Prophet Muhammad.
parapet	A narrow protective wall built on top of the main wall of a fort. Soldiers could stand on the main wall and hide behind the parapet.
pike	A long, sharp, pointed spear used for thrusting at an enemy.
pilgrim	A visitor to a holy place, such as Jerusalem.
Reeve	A man of high rank who acted as a kind of overseer for the king.
villein	A peasant of the Middle Ages. Villeins worked on the land to support themselves and the landowners.

Index

This index is an alphabetical list of the important words and topics in this book.

When you are looking for a special piece of information, you can look for the word in the list and it will tell you which pages to look at.

Acknowledgement

The publishers of **Childcraft** gratefully acknowledge the following artists, photographers, publishers, agencies and corporations for illustrations used in this volume. All illustrations are the exclusive property of the publishers of **Childcraft** unless names are marked with an asterisk*.

Cover	Trevor Ridley, B. L. Kearley Limited
6/7	Hemesh Alles, Maggie Mundy Artists Agency
8/9	Trevor Ridley, B. L. Kearley Limited
10/11	Barry Wilkinson, B. L. Kearley Limited
12/13	Donald Harley, B. L. Kearley Limited
14/15	Michael Strand, B. L. Kearley Limited
16/17	Roger Wade Walker, Specs Art Agency
18/19	Roy King, Specs Art Agency
20/21	Richard Berridge
22/23	Trevor Ridley, B. L. Kearley Limited
24/25	Sharon Pallent, Maggie Mundy Artists Agency
26/27	Roger Jones, Specs Art Agency
28/29	Donald Harley, B. L. Kearley Limited
30/31	Barry Wilkinson, B. L. Kearley Limited
32/33	Trevor Ridley, B. L. Kearley Limited
34/35	Sharon Pallent, Maggie Mundy Artists Agency
36/37	Richard Berridge
38/39	Mark Peppé, B. L. Kearley Limited
40/41	Roy King, Specs Art Agency
42/43	Donald Harley, B. L. Kearley Limited
44/45	Richard Berridge
46/47	Roger Jones, Specs Art Agency
48/49	Terry Thomas, Specs Art Agency
50/51	Richard Berridge
52/53	Charles Front
54/55	Trevor Ridley, B. L. Kearley Limited
56/57	Mark Peppé, B. L. Kearley Limited
58/59	Terry Thomas, Specs Art Agency
60/61	Richard Berridge
62/63	Charles Front
64/65	Donald Harley, B. L. Kearley Limited
66/67	Roy King, Specs Art Agency
68/69	Michael Strand, B. L. Kearley Limited
70/71	Tony Chance, Specs Art Agency
72/73	Barry Wilkinson, B. L. Kearley Limited
74/75	Mark Peppé, B. L. Kearley Limited
76/77	Richard Berridge
78/79	Terry Thomas, Specs Art Agency
80/81	Donald Harley, B. L. Kearley Limited
82/83	Roy King, Specs Art Agency
84/85	Shirley Bellwood, B. L. Kearley Limited
86/87	Charles Front
88/89	Trevor Ridley, B. L. Kearley Limited
90/91	Michael Strand, B. L. Kearley Limited
92/93	Tony Chance, Specs Art Agency
94/95	Trevor Ridley, B. L. Kearley Limited
96/97	Mark Peppé, B. L. Kearley Limited
98/99	Charles Front
100/101	Michael Strand, B. L. Kearley Limited
102/103	Trevor Ridley, B. L. Kearley Limited
104/105	Richard Berridge
106/107	Trevor Ridley, B. L. Kearley Limited
108/109	Michael Strand, B. L. Kearley Limited
110/111	Mark Peppé, B. L. Kearley Limited
112/113	Charles Front
114/115	Roy King, Specs Art Agency
116/117	Mark Peppé, B. L. Kearley Limited
118/119	Michael Strand, B. L. Kearley Limited
120/121	Charles Front
122/123	Dermot Power, B. L. Kearley Limited
124/125	Richard Berridge
126/127	Trevor Ridley, B. L. Kearley Limited
128/129	Tony Chance, Specs Art Agency
130/131	Richard Berridge
132/133	Trevor Ridley, B. L. Kearley Limited
134/135	Terry Thomas, Specs Art Agency
136/137	Roy King, Specs Art Agency
138/138	Lynne Byrnes, Maggie Mundy
140/141	Michael Strand, B. L. Kearley Limited
142/143	Charles Front
144/145	Richard Berridge
146/147	Shirley Bellwood, B. L. Kearley Limited
148/149	Trevor Ridley, B. L. Kearley Limited
150/151	Ian Botham, Virginia Wade, Sebastian Coe, (All-Sport Photographic*), Gareth Edwards, (Colorsport*), World Cup, (Syndication International Ltd*)
152/153	Crown jewels, (HMSO*), St. Paul's, (ZEFA Picture Library*), Heathrow, (Spectrum Colour Library*), St. Katherine's, (Bruce Coleman Ltd*)